700 Real Christian Names

Choosing a name for your baby

Tony Castle

Augsburg Books
MINNEAPOLIS

700 REAL CHRISTIAN NAMES
Choosing a name for your baby

© Copyright 2009 Tony Castle

Original edition published in English under the title 700 REAL CHRISTIAN NAMES by Kevin Mayhew Ltd, Buxhall, England.

This edition published in 2020 by Fortress Press. All rights reserved. Except for brief quotations in critical articles or reviews, no part of this book may be reproduced in any manner without prior written permission from the publisher. Email copyright@augsburgfortress.org or write to Permissions, Fortress Press, PO Box 1209, Minneapolis, MN 55440-1209.

Cover image: © iStock 2020: Green Baby Shoe stock photo by Floortje
Cover design: Emily Drake

Print ISBN: 978-1-5064-5978-3

Contents

About the author		5	
Introduction		7	

Boys		Girls	
A	13	A	111
B	23	B	118
C	29	C	123
D	39	D	133
E	43	E	138
F	49	F	144
G	53	G	146
H	57	H	150
I	60	I	153
J	62	J	155
K	70	K	160
L	72	L	162
M	77	M	166
N	84	N	175
O	87	O	177
P	89	P	178
Q	92	R	181
R	93	S	184
S	97	T	188
T	101	U	191
V	104	V	192
W	106	W	194
X	108	Y	195
Z	108	Z	196

For my grandchildren:
Charlotte, Emily, Joel and Catherine.

About the author

Recently retired from teaching, as Head of Religious Studies, Tony Castle is currently a Diocesan Inspector of Catholic schools and Director of the Catholic Certificate in Religious Studies for the Diocese of Brentwood.

He is an international writer of over 50 educational, liturgical and spiritual books, which have been published in several languages, including Portuguese, Polish, Chinese and Hungarian. His best known *Quotes and Anecdotes for Preachers and Teachers* has been in print, and sought after, for the past 30 years.

Introduction

In the past 50 years there has been a virtual explosion of new forenames augmenting the stock of well-established traditional ones. The multi-ethnic and multi-cultural nature of modern Britain has also swelled the pool of names to choose from and led to the demise of referring to a person's first name as his or her 'Christian' name. For nearly 1500 years, throughout Christian Europe, names were bestowed at Baptism and were referred to as 'baptismal' or 'Christian' names.

For every serious, committed Christian, Baptism, or as it is also known, Christening, is much more than a naming ceremony; it is the most important, once-in-a-lifetime event, when they or their child enter into a very special relationship with God and become a member of the universal Church. In times past, this was marked and kept in memory by the bestowal of a name taken from the Bible or one of the renowned and revered members of the family of Jesus that we call 'the Church'.

Over the centuries, social, political and religious upheavals have influenced the forenames given at birth; for example, the Normans brought many new names into England after the Conquest of 1066. Again, the seventeenth-century Puritans, who would have no truck with following the ancient tradition of using saints' names, searched the Bible for new biblical names.

The tradition of keeping your 'name day', the special day associated with the saint you are named after (the feast day of the saint) was killed off by the Puritans and replaced by celebrating 'birth days' instead. Not so long ago, in Christian countries like Poland, 'name days' were still kept and only gradually have birthdays become a popular replacement.

In this book I have given the reader the opportunity of knowing, and perhaps using again, the 'name day' associated with the forename. After each name, where applicable, the 'special day' (shown in italics) of the saint is given. Where it is known, this is usually the day on which the holy person died or was 'born into heaven'; failing that, it is the traditional date given to them on the Christian calendar. While I am not expecting a nationwide revival of a good ancient practice, there may be a parent or two who, having chosen a traditional Christian name for their child, would like them to know and celebrate their own special name day.

Another tradition is that of a 'family name', which may or may not be, strictly speaking, a 'Christian' name. My own two forenames illustrate both practices. The first entails a story. When my mother was expecting her first child, my father lost his job as a butcher, because he dared to ask for a rise in salary as my mother was just about to leave her secretarial post to have the baby. (No maternity grants or leave in those days!) Suddenly both were unemployed during a period of widespread unemployment. There appeared to be no jobs about, but my mother, being a devout Catholic, started to pray and she asked her favourite saint, St Anthony of Padua, to add his prayers to hers. She promised that if God heard their prayers, she would name her baby after him. On the fourth day of the nine-day Novena of prayer, a stranger stopped my father in the street and asked him if he was looking for employment. My father took the job (driving heavy transport) and happily remained with the same company until his retirement: and I became 'Anthony'!

My second name is a family name, 'Percy', borne by my father and his father before him. However, as I have never liked it, it was not inflicted upon our son; his second name is 'Anthony'. This brings us to the importance of choosing a name for a child; it is one of the most important decisions that parents make for the child at the time of birth. The bestowal of a personal name for life, is a serious responsibility requiring careful thought and consideration. The name a child is known by, and called, can effect that child's self-perception and the perception of others. One or both parents liking a particular name, is not sufficient reason for using it; there are many considerations to take into account; for example, how does it sound with the surname (jokes abound about unthinking combinations, e.g. Teresa Green – trees-a-green); how do the initials look together, some, like B.O.G. might not make life pleasant in the playground!

As a practical guide for parents I have kept the entries short and simple; answering the immediate questions: What does the name mean? Where does it originate from? What are its Christian roots or how does it come to be a Christian name?

The opening of the twenty-first century has seen an interesting revival in boys names from the Bible; for example, Joshua, Adam, Joel, Noah. While among the girls, names like Faith, Hope, Grace etc have made a comeback. It is reassuring to witness traditional names once again challenging names taken from popular celebrities. May 'Elizabeth' and 'Mary', 'Thomas' and 'Peter' be as popular in a century's time as they have been for the last nineteen centuries.

Tony Castle

Boys

A

Aaron

The name is probably Egyptian and its meaning is unknown. It was bestowed upon the elder brother of Moses while the Hebrews were captive in Egypt; he became the first High Priest of Israel (Exodus 6:13). There was also a sixth-century Celtic saint of this name. He lived as a hermit in Brittany; one of his disciples was St Malo. The name has been in regular use in the Jewish community for centuries. It was adopted by Nonconformist Christians in the seventeenth century.

22 June

Abel

The meaning of this name, probably derived from the Hebrew, is obscure and may originate from *'ablu'* meaning 'son'. One of the first names found in the Bible, Abel was the second son of Adam and Eve, murdered by his brother Cain (Genesis 4:1–16). It was traditionally used in the Christian litany for the dying. Popular among the seventeenth-century Puritans, it is not much used in the twenty-first century.

2 January

Abner

From the Hebrew, meaning 'father of light'. Abner is found in the Bible (1 Samuel 20:25) as the cousin of King Saul and commander of his army. While never popular in England, from the time of the Pilgrim Fathers, it has been frequently used in the USA.

Abraham

From the Hebrew (in its original form of 'Abram' meaning 'high father') it was changed to Abraham (Genesis 12) meaning 'father of multitudes'. He was the patriarch, founder of the Jewish faith and progenitor of the Hebrew nation. Seven Christian saints, all rather obsure hermits or monks of the fourth–seventh centuries, bore the name. Always popular in Jewish usage; it only found general use in England among the Puritans of the seventeenth century. It is popular nowadays in many Christian parts of Africa.

9 October

Achilles

Although Greek in origin, the meaning is obscure; the name of this Homeric hero was rarely used in Christian Europe, although there is one little known fourth-century saint (a). It was also the name of one of the Ugandan martyrs executed for the Christian faith in 1886 (b).

(a) 15 May, (b) 3 June

Adam

Of uncertain origin it, probably comes from the Hebrew word *'adama'* meaning 'earth'; and as such was the name given to the first man who came from the earth (Genesis 2:4–25). There are two thirteenth-century saints, both monks, of this name. At that period it was one of the most common names in England; it lost its popularity for several hundred years, but it has returned to frequent use in modern times.

24 December

Adlai

The name of a very minor biblical character (1 Chronicles 27:29) popularised by seventeenth-century Puritans. It was taken to North America by the Pilgrim Fathers and is still popular in the USA.

Adrian

This is the English form of the Latin name *'Hadrianus'* (a man from Hadria, a town in northern Italy). The name of a Roman Emperor and several popes. The only English pope, Nicholas Breakspear (d.1159) took the name Adrian IV. There have been eight saints of this name. The most famous was a Benedictine monk and headmaster of St Augustine's school, Canterbury; he died in 710.

9 January

Aelred

This is a version of the Saxon name Ethelred. He left the service of King David of Scotland for a more austere life and became a Cistercian monk in about 1134, at the great monastery of Rievaulx, Yorkshire. He rose to become abbot. Famed for his preaching and asceticism, he was hailed a saint in his own lifetime.

3 February

Alan

There are several variants of this Celtic name e.g. 'Alun', 'Alein' and 'Allen'. Its meaning is not certain, but 'harmony' has been suggested. There was a popular Welsh saint of this name in the fifth century. The name (then spelt 'Alain') became established and popular in England as a result of the Norman Conquest.

26 October

Alban

The name of one of the first British martyrs (fourth century) for the Christian faith, who died at Verulamium, now known as St Albans. He offered himself for execution to allow a Roman soldier (some say a priest) to escape. Never very popular, the name was briefly fashionable in the nineteenth century, when the variants 'Albany' and 'Albion' were in use.

20 June

Alberic

This comes from the Old German 'Albirich'. There were four saints of the Benedictine Order of this name; the best known, of the twelfth century, was one of the three founders of the Cistercian Order.

26 January

Albert

Comes from the French, but it is Germanic in origin; it was brought to England by the Normans. It was popular in the nineteenth century to honour Queen Victoria's husband, Prince Albert. It means 'noble' and 'virtuous'. Very popular among the saints, there are twenty-one with this name; the most famous was Albert the Great (1200–80), a brilliant theologian and the teacher of Thomas Aquinas. He was declared a Doctor of the Church (RC) in 1931.

15 November

Alcuin

French in origin, the meaning is obscure. St Alcuin was a monk of Northumbria who became adviser to the Emperor Charlemagne. Renowned for his learning (his poetry and prayers have survived the centuries) he became abbot of a famous monastery at Tours. Not a popular name in modern times.

19 May

Aldhem

Probably a Saxon name, Aldhem (639–709) was a member of the Wessex royal family. He became a Benedictine monk at Canterbury, but returned to Malmesbury, as director of the school there. He established several monasteries and acted as adviser to King Ine of the West Saxons; he ended his days as the first bishop of Sherborne. He is considered the first English scholar of distinction.

25 May

Alexander

A popular name in the post-classical period, this derives from the fame of Alexander the Great. Several New Testament characters and a host of early Christian martyrs bore the name. The most recent saint is Alexander Briant, a Jesuit priest, executed at Tyburn in 1581. The name means 'helper and protector of man'.

1 December

Alexis

From 'Alexius' (Latin version of the Greek 'Alexios') derived from *'alexein'* meaning 'to defend'. St Alexius lived in the fifth century, his life is surrounded by legend; venerated in the Orthodox Church, the name is common in Russia. In the West it has also been given to girls.

17 July

Alfred

Comes from the Old English, AEkfaed, meaning 'wise counsel of the elf'. Alfred the Great (849–899) was King of Wessex, patron of learning, defender of the Church against the Danes and venerated in Christian England as a saint. He was regarded as the pattern of Christian kingship. The name, in various forms, spread widely throughout Europe; popular in the nineteenth century, its use has waned in recent times.

26 October

Aloysius *(also Ludovicus)*

The Latin form of the French name 'Louis'. Two saints have borne this name; the most famous, especially in Roman Catholic circles, is the sixteenth-century Aloysius Gonzaga, a member of the Society of Jesus (Jesuits), who died from nursing plague victims when he was only twenty-two. Canonised in 1726, he was declared patron of Catholic Youth in the twentieth century.

21 June

Alphonsus

Originally a German name meaning 'noble and ready', it was taken to Spain, where it became a favourite name as 'Alphonso', 'Alfonso' or 'Alonso'. Not surprisingly, it was the name of nine Spanish saints. However, the most famous saint of this name was from Naples, Italy. Alphonsus Ligouri (1696–1787) was a theologian, bishop and founder of the Redemptorist Congregation of Priests.

1 August

Amadeus

From the two Latin words 'amo' and 'Deus', meaning 'lover of God'. There are three little known saints of this name. It is occasionally used in African circles.

10 August

Amasa

Of Hebrew origin, meaning 'burden bearer'. A captain of Absalom's army (2 Samuel 19:13) who succeeded Joab as David's commander-in-chief. Occasionally used in Puritan times.

Ambrose

This is the English form of the Latin 'Ambrosius' meaning 'immortal'. Twelve saints sprinkled through history bore this name; the most illustrious was Ambrose, the fourth-century Bishop of Milan. Famous for his preaching and for being one of the greatest bishops of Christian history, he is credited with the conversion of the great Augustine of Hippo.

7 December

Amos

A Hebrew name, probably from the verb *'amos'*, to carry. This has been interpreted by some to mean 'borne by God'. The name of one of the minor Old Testament prophets; the book of the Bible named after him, carries references to his life as a shepherd and dresser of sycamore trees. Although not much used in modern Britain, it was popular among the Puritans and retains some popularity in the USA.

31 March

Andreas

The original Greek form of 'Andrew', sometimes used as a variant *(see Andrew)*.

Andrew

A popular European name that appears in several variants; it comes from the Greek for 'manly'. According to John's gospel, Andrew was the first disciple to be called by Jesus, to whom he introduced his brother Simon Peter. The apostle Andrew was a very popular saint in medieval Europe; he was adopted as patron saint of Russia, Greece and Scotland. His emblem in art is the traditional X-shaped cross of his martyrdom (he was supposedly crucified at Patras, Achaia). Twenty-one other Christian saints bear this name.

30 November

Anselm

An Old German name meaning 'divine helmet'. It was chiefly used by Lombards and it was St Anselm (1033–1109), a Lombard, who first brought the name to England when he was appointed Archbishop of Canterbury. A brilliant scholar, he had a stormy career opposing the demands of the English monarch. Never really popular in Britain, it enjoyed a revival of interest in the nineteenth century.

21 April

Antony *(Anthony)*

A well-established European name (meaning 'of inestimable worth'), that comes from the Greek, 'Anthonios' or the Latin 'Antonius'; hence there are two versions of the name, one with, and one without, the 'h'. The early popularity of the name is due to St Antony (251-356), the first Christian hermit, then a monk, who lived in Egypt (a). The name's later popularity is due to the fame of St Anthony of Padua, (1195–1231) a gifted Franciscan preacher, who died at Padua, Italy (b). He is famously invoked to help find lost objects; represented in art carrying the child Jesus. There are host of other lesser-known saints of the same name.

(a) 17 January, (b) 13 June

Archibald

Originates from the Old German 'Ercanbald' and means 'noble' and 'truly bold'. There was no biblical character or saint of this name, but it entered Christian usage because of the Anglo-Saxon, pre-Conquest, St Eorkonweald (d.693) who was sometimes referred to as St Archibald. It was used in the north of England and was particularly popular in Scotland.

Armel

From the old Breton 'Arzhel 'meaning 'bear prince'. It was the name of a sixth-century monk, who travelled from Wales to Brittany to join a monastery there. In later life he founded several monasteries and was, according to legend, well-known for the power of his prayers.

16 August

Arnold

Comes from the Old German 'Arenvald', meaning 'strong as an eagle'. The Normans brought the name to England as 'Arnaud'. The original saint (there are two others) was a Greek (d.800) who was famous for his charity to the poor.

8 July

Asa

A biblical name (see 1 Kings 15:9-23) borne by a King of Judah, son of Abijah, who reigned for forty years. Of Hebrew origin, the name means 'doctor' or 'healer'. Apart from Jewish usage, it was used in Christian circles in the seventeenth century by the Puritans; only rarely in the twentieth century.

Asaph

Of Hebrew origin, meaning 'collector'. There are two variants 'Asaf' and 'Asiph'. The saint of this name lived in the early seventh century and was a follower of St Kentigern, who founded a monastery with over 900 members in north Wales. Asaph became the leader of the community and bishop. Today, St Asaph's cathedral stands on the site.

4 May

Augustine *(also Austin)*

A popular name throughout Europe, particularly in England, during the Middle Ages when the 'Austin' form was in common use. It comes from the Latin 'Augustus' meaning 'venerable'. There are nine saints of this name, the most influential in history was Augustine of Hippo (fourth century), one of the greatest theologians of the Western Church (a). In England, the popularity of the name more probably came from the Augustine, who was the first Archbishop of Canterbury (sixth century) and brought Christianity to Kent and the south of England (b).

(a) 28 August, (b) 27 May

B

Baldwin

Germanic in origin, the name meaning 'bold friend', became popular in Flanders and was introduced into England by the Normans. There was a lesser-known Benedictine saint of the twelfth century, but no other particular Christian usage is recorded. Though less common in modern times, it has not completely disappeared.

15 July

Baptist

Originating from the Latin *'baptista'* (one who baptises) the name is usually used along with 'John' (so, 'John-Baptist'). Although uncommon in either form in Britain, it is much used in Roman Catholic countries and among some evangelical sects in the USA.

Barnabas

Hebrew in origin, the name means 'son of consolation'. A travelling companion of St Paul, Barnabas was never an Apostle, but because of the many references to him in the New Testament, he has always been honoured as one. Tradition has it that he died a martyr in Cyprus. In art he is always depicted as standing near a pile of stones and holding a book. The name has been used in Britain since about 1200; however, the variants 'Barnaby', 'Barnabe' or 'Barney' have been more commonly used.

11 June

Barnard *(See Bernard).*

Bartholomew

This is the name of one of the twelve Apostles; it is Hebrew in origin, meaning 'son of Talmai' or 'son of the furrows'. In the New Testament he is also known as 'Nathaniel'. The name was very common in England and throughout Europe from the twelfth century onwards, which is attested by there being thirteen other saints of this name.

24 August

Baruch

A biblical name of Hebrew origin meaning 'blessed'. It was the name of the prophet Jeremiah's secretary and companion (Jeremiah 32:12) also of two lesser-known characters (see Nehemiah 3:20 and Nehemiah 10:6). Used as a Christian name from the sixteenth century, especially in the English Midlands; but not common this last century.

Basil

From the Greek, meaning 'kingly'. It is a popular name throughout the Eastern Christian Church due to the reverence given to St Basil the Great (c.330–379), Bishop of Caesarea and theologian. He is considered one of the three founding Fathers of the Eastern Church and one of the four great doctors (eminent teachers) of the Western (Latin) Church. There were several other lesser-known saints of this name. It was used in England from the end of the twelfth century; its use lapsed but was revived in the nineteenth century, mainly in the High Church of the Church of England.

2 January

Bede

From the Anglo-Saxon word for 'prayer'. Although not common in modern times, it was a popular name in the Middle Ages, due to the respect for St Bede (d.735) or the Venerable Bede – the monk of Jarrow, in Northumbria, who was a famed scholar and writer. He has the accolade of the first English historian because of his invaluble *Ecclesiastical History of the English People*.

25 May

Benedict

Very popular thoroughout the Middle Ages (there are twenty-one saints of this name) it comes from the Latin 'Benedictus' meaning 'blessed' or ' one blessed by God'. Its popularity springs from the saint (480–550) who founded the famous Benedictine Order of monks and gave the Christian world a model of a monastic rule and life. He began as a hermit at Subiaco, central Italy, gathered many followers and moved to Monte Cassino, where he founded the great monastery (site of a great World War II battle). His life and work is considered one of the most powerful factors in the building up on civilisation in Christian Europe. He was declared patron of Europe in 1964.

11 July

Benjamin

This name appears three times in the Bible (Genesis 35:18; 1 Chronicles 7:10; Ezra 10:32) but it usually calls to mind the youngest son of Jacob. He was first named 'Benoni' meaning 'son of sorrow' by his mother Rachel, who died shortly after his birth. However, his father renamed him 'Benjamin' meaning 'son of the south'. More usually a Jewish name, it was used as a

Christian name in Britain after the Reformation; declined in use during the nineteenth century but it returned to popularity in the late twentieth century (short form –Ben). There was one rather obscure saint of this name who died a martyr in 421.

31 March

Bernard

Originates from the Old German 'Berinhard' meaning 'brave as bear'. Used throughout the Continent (witness twelve European saints of this name) it became particularly popular due to the influence of two renowned saints: St Bernard of Methon (d.1081) who for forty years served travellers in the Alps, founding two hospices in the passes that bear his name. The famous rescue-dog is also named after him (a). St Bernard of Clairvaux (1090–1153) influential founder of the Cisterician Order (he founded sixty-eight monasteries) theologian, writer and adviser of popes, kings and Church councils (b). Use of the name declined at the Reformation, (the Reformers would not name their children after saints!) but experienced a revival in the nineteenth century. The diminutive 'Bernie' is used in the USA.

(a) 28 May, (b) 20 August

Bertram

Some claim this name to be, in origin, an Anglo-Saxon name, others Old French or Germanic; its meaning is 'bright raven'. It was certainly used in England after the Norman Conquest in several varied forms, 'Bertran', 'Bartram' or 'Bertrand'; with the diminutive, 'Bertie'. There are two obscure Christian saints of the seventh and eighth centuries who bore the name.

24 January or 6 September

Blaise (Blase)

Probably comes from the Latin *'blaesus'*, meaning 'stammerer'. It was a very popular name in medieval England because St Blaise, Bishop of Sebaste, martyred in 316 was patron saint of the influential wool-makers. Legend has it that he saved the life of a boy who was choking on a fish bone. In the Roman Catholic Church there is a traditional annual blessing of throats on his feast day.

3 February

Blane

Of Gaelic origin, the name means 'yellow'. There is one Scottish saint of this name (d.590) who was born on the island of Bute, and studied in Ireland where he became a monk and eventually bishop. He returned to Scotland where he dedicated himself to missionary work. The Dunblane cathedral is built on the site of a monastery he founded. There is the variant of the name, 'Blayne'; both are sometimes used for girls.

11 August

Boniface

From the Latin *'bonifacius'* meaning 'one who does good'. Not common nowadays, it was, however, very popular in England from the thirteenth century to the Reformation. The original saint was a third-century Christian martyred at Tarsus; besides a series of popes, twelve later saints bore the name. The most important, by far, was the Anglo-Saxon Benedictine monk (680–754) who took Christianity to Germany and gained the title 'the Apostle of the Germans'.

5 June

Brendan

A Gaelic name derived from *'breaninn'* meaning 'prince'. The modern Irish form (where it is frequently used) 'Breanden' and the English version are based on Latin 'Brendanus'. There were two sixth-century saints, Brendan the Navigator, or Voyager, who is believed to be the first European to sail to North America (a); and Brendan of Birr (b). The first is one of the three most famous saints of Ireland and the patron of sailors.

(a) 16 May, (b) 29 November

Brice

Of Celtic origin, the name means 'quick' and 'ambitious'. It was much in vogue in England and France during the Middle Ages due to St Brice, Bishop of Tours (d.444), a popular disciple of the great St Martin of Tours.

13 November

Bruno

From the German *'brun'* meaning 'brown'. The existence of five saints of this name in the tenth–eleventh centuries attest to its wide use throughout the whole of Europe in the Middle Ages. The most prominent saint being the son of the Emperor Henry the Fowler, who was Archbishop of Cologne (a). Another was Bruno of Chartreuse, the founder of the Carthusian Order who died in 1101 (b).

(a) 11 October, (b) 6 October

C

Caleb

A biblical name from the Hebrew meaning 'bold' or 'impetuous'; it appears twice in the Bible. The son of Hezron (1 Chronicles 2:18) and the better-known son of Jephunneh (Numbers 13:6) who spied out the Promised Land for Joshua. He alone, of the original Hebrew slaves to leave Egypt, enters the Promised Land with Joshua (Numbers 26:65). The name was popular in Puritan times and taken by them to the USA where it is still in use.

Calum

This name originates from the Latin word *'columba'* meaning 'dove', via the Scottish-Gaelic tradition. It was very popular in early Christian times because of the symbolism of the dove representing peace, gentleness and the Holy Spirit. The great St Columba was the most famous of the saints of Scotland. He founded many monasteries in Ireland and Scotland and is revered as the missionary of the north and the founder of the monastery on Iona.

9 June

Calvin

The name originates from the French surname of the Protestant Reformer and theologian, Jean Calvin (1509–64), used mainly in the USA by Christians of the Reformed tradition. As a surname the name meant 'little bald one'.

Carl

Increasingly popular in the English-speaking world, it is a variant of 'Karl', which is the German version of Charles *(see Charles)*.

Casimir

Of Slavic origin, the name means 'proclaimer of peace'. St Casimir was a fifteenth-century Polish prince who resisted the evil political plans of his father. As patron of Poland and Lithuania, the name is found mostly among Roman Catholics of Eastern European origins.

4 March

Caspar

A Persian name meaning 'master of the treasure'. It is one of the legendary names given to the Magi who journeyed from the east to visit the child Jesus (Matthew 2:1). The Bible, however, does not record how many there were or their names. Several saints and holy persons, particularly of the seventeenth century were named after the legendary figure. Variants are 'Jasper' (Dutch form) and 'Casper'.

6 January

Cassian

The name originates from a Latin clan the 'Cassianus' (the word meaning 'empty' or 'hollow'). There were several early, quite obscure, saints, but the most eminent was the monk and theologian, John Cassian, who was never honoured as a saint in the Western Church.

23 July

Cathal

An Irish name for 'Charles' or 'Carl' derived from the Old Celtic words for 'battle' and 'ruler'. It was borne by the seventeenth-century Irish saint who originated from Munster but became, eventually, Bishop of Taranto in Italy. Variants are 'Cathaldus' and 'Cataldus'.

10 May

Cedd

An Anglo-Saxon name, the meaning of which is unclear. St Cedd (d.664) was a monk of Lindisfarne who was sent south to evangelise the East Saxons. He set up many religious communities including Bradwell, Essex, where he is remembered and venerated every year. He was the first bishop of the East Saxons but was recalled to Yorkshire where he died.

26 October

Chad

Like his older brother Cedd *(above)*, Chad had an Anglo-Saxon name and was trained at Lindisfarne. He replaced his brother, when he died, as abbot at Lastingham, and later became bishop of the huge diocese of Mercia. Like his brother he died (672) of the plague, rampant at that time.

2 March

Charles

A popular European name with many variants, e.g. 'Carl', 'Carlos', 'Carol', 'Karol', 'Cary'. It originates from the German word meaning 'free man'. Its popularity sprang at first from the Frankish leader, Charles the Great, or Charlemagne, who in 800 became the

Holy Roman Emperor. The Church confirmed popular devotion by allowing the Emperor the title 'Blessed'. There followed eight other saintly men, the most famous being Charles Borromeo (1538–84) the influential Counter-Reformation Bishop of Milan. The name was introduced into England by Mary Queen of Scots and so became established as a royal name.

4 November

Chris

Short form of 'Christopher' and other associated names *(see Christopher)*.

Christian

From the Latin 'Christianus' the name first given to the followers of Christ at Antioch (see Acts 11:26) about the year 60, previously called 'The People of the Way'. The word 'Christian' is the Greek equivalent of the Hebrew word 'Messiah' meaning 'anointed'. Used as a given name in Britain, from time to time, since the twelfth century. The only saint of this name was a twelfth-century Irish bishop of Clogher.

12 June

Christopher

A popular European name, it comes from the Greek meaning 'the Christ-bearer'. It was originally a word used by Christians and applied to themselves, meaning that they bore Christ by faith in their hearts. There was an obscure early Christian martyr who died at Lycia in Roman times. His name has attracted many legends, the most beautiful is the commonly known story that he carried an unknown child across a flooded ford; the child was Christ. The story led to the usual representation of the saint in art and popular devotion. The patron saint of travellers, in Roman Catholic countries, he is regarded particularly as the patron of motorists. One of the most popular of the medieval saints, his name is used widely throughout Europe.

25 July

Ciaran

An Irish-Gaelic name that has been translated in England as 'Kieran'; it means 'small and dark-skinned'. Two sixth-century Irish saints who helped in the conversion of Ireland to Christianity bore this name.

5 March or 9 September

Cillian

Recognised in English as 'Kilian' or 'Killian'; it is a Gaelic name meaning 'little warlike one'. There were three seventh-century Irish saints of this name.

8 or 29 July

Claude

This is the French version of the Latin name 'Claudius', which is derived from *'claudus'* meaning 'lame'. There were seven early Christian martyrs (third and fourth centuries) of this name, but its popularity in France is due to St Claude of Besancon, a seventh-century abbot and bishop.

6 June

Claus

German version of 'Nicholas' (*see Nicholas*).

Clem

Short form of 'Clement' *(see Clement)*.

Clement

Derived from the Latin *'clemens'* meaning 'merciful'; this was a very popular Christian name, borne throughout history by thirteen very different saints. St Clement I (d.99) was the third successor of St Peter in the See of Rome; there were thirteen other popes of the same name, the last being in the eighteenth century.

23 November

Colin

This comes from the French diminutive of 'Col', short for 'Nicholas'. It means 'strong and virile'. The name is found in England from the thirteenth century and gave rise to the surnames 'Collins' and 'Collinson'. The Scottish 'Colin' comes from a different root: it is believed that it comes from the Gaelic 'Cailean', which relates to St Columba.

(St Nicolas) 6 December, (St Columba) 9 June

Colman

The name originates from Northern Ireland and most of the seven saints of that name (Gaelic word derived from 'charcoal burner') lived there or in Scotland. The best known was the sixth century, Colman of Dromore, who founded a monastery and was eventually bishop of that place. While the name is occasionally found in the USA, it is not popular in modern Britain.

7 June

Colum *(Colm)*

The Irish form of 'Columba', from the Latin for 'dove'. St Columba (521–597) was the missionary who took the Christian faith to the Picts of northern England and Scotland. He is more usually known by the name 'Columcille'.

9 June

Conan

Derived from the Old Celtic meaning 'high and mighty'. There were several obscure Irish saints of this name, the better known being the seventh-century monk of Iona who became the first bishop in the Isle of Man.

26 January

Conrad

The English version of the German name 'Konrad' meaning 'brave counsellor'. There were five saints of this name, the most prominent being Conrad of Constance, a tenth-century bishop. Essentially a German name, it has occasionally been used in Britain, particularly from the nineteenth century.

26 November

Cormac

An ancient Irish name, commonly found in Irish myths and legends; it is of uncertain origin and meaning. Two Irish saints bore the name, the most famous being the tenth-century first bishop of Cashel.

14 September

Cornelius

Originating from an old Roman family name, it probably means 'horn'. This was the name of the devout Roman centurion, stationed at Caesarea, first century Palastine, who was converted by Peter (see Acts 10:1–40). Also the name of a third-century martyred pope and three other, rather obscure, saints. Used throughout Europe, it has been particularly popular in the Netherlands.

16 September

Cosmo (*Cosmas*)

This is the Italian version of the Greek name 'Kosmas' which means 'order'. Several saints bear this name, the most well-known being one of the twins Cosmas and Damien. They were medical doctors who gave their services to the poor for nothing and died as martyrs under the Emperor Diocletian (c.303). They were very popular throughout Europe during the Middle Ages and many beautiful legends of caring for the sick grew up around them. The name was brought to Britain in the eighteenth century, but has never proved popular.

26 September

Crispin (*Crispian*)

From the Latin 'Crispinus', a Roman name, probably meaning 'curly-headed'. Very popular in medieval times, there are seven saints with this name. The first, and most popular, was the shoemaker (hence St Crispin is the patron of shoemakers) who died a martyr's death at Soissons, France, about 285.

25 October

Cuthbert

Although now out of fashion, this was a common Old English name (meaning 'bright and famous') from before the Norman Conquest. Two bishop-saints bore the name; Cuthbert of Lindisfarne (d.687) one of the most famous English saints, whose tomb at Durham was a popular place of pilgrimage where many miracles were recorded (a). Cuthbert, Archbishop of Canterbury (d.758) of whom little is known. Modern Roman Catholics recall St Cuthbert Mayne (1544–1577), who was executed at Launceston for celebrating Mass when it was a crime to do so, under Elizabeth I (b).

(a) 4 September, (b) 29 November.

Cyprian

From the Latin 'Cyprianus' meaning 'native of Cyprus'. The great St Cyprian of Carthage (200–258) was one of the first important Christian writers. He wrote several important books and was beheaded during the Diocletian persecution of Christians. Several less-distinguished saints bear the same name.

16 September

Cyril

Probably from the Greek word *'kyrios'* meaning 'lord'. It was a popular name among the early Christians, attested by the twelve saints of the early centuries. In addition the famous theologians and teachers, Cyril of Jerusalem (d.386) (a) and Cyril of Alexandria (d.444) (b); there was also St Cyril, 'the Apostle of the Slavs' (d.869) (c), who with his brother, Methodius, took

CYRIL

Christianity to the Slavonic regions of Eastern Europe. The name does not appear to have been used in Britain before the seventeenth century; it was very popular in the nineteenth century but rarely found nowadays.

(a) 18 March, (b) 27 June, (c) 14 February

Dafydd
The Welsh form of David *(see David)*.

Damien
Probably derived from the Greek word *'daman'* meaning 'to tame'; the name may also be taken from the Greek classical name, 'Damon'. There are several lesser-known saints, however, the best known is the brother of St Cosmas *(see Cosmos)*. Modern Roman Catholics are more likely to associate the name with Father Damien (1840–1889), the heroic missionary to the lepers of Molokai, a Pacific island. (He was declared 'Blessed' in 1995). The name was in regular use in Britain from the thirteenth century.

10 May

Dan
This can be a shortened version of 'Daniel' or a name in its own right. It is a Hebrew word meaning 'he judged' and was the name given to Jacob's son by Bilhah, Rachel's maid (Genesis 30:6).

Daniel
A Hebrew word meaning 'the Lord is my judge'. There are two Daniels in the Bible; the first was the son of David and Abigail (1 Chronicles 3:1); the second, Daniel the prophet, is the most important. His story is found in the Book of Daniel. The tale of him in the lions' den was very popular in medieval miracle plays, so the

name was widely used throughout Europe. There are eight Christian saints bearing the name, none of great note or fame. Used in England from before the Norman Conquest, it went out of vogue in the nineteenth century, but in recent times it has returned to popularity.

21 July

Darius

The masculine form of 'Daria'. There was a St Daria who died at Rome for Christian faith in 283, with her Egyptian husband, Chrysanthus; they are buried on the Via Salaria.

25 October

David

Originally this was a Hebrew lullaby word meaning 'darling', then later, 'friend' or 'beloved'. This was one of the titles of the great King David, beloved of God, shepherd-son of Jesse, who succeeded Saul as King of Judah and Israel (a). He is credited with many of the psalms and is one of the types of Christ in the Old Testament. His story is told in 1 and 2 Samuel. One of the first bearers of the name in Britain was Dewi, or David, Archbishop of Menevia (d.600); patron saint of Wales (b). From his time, the name has been a favourite one in Wales, although never very popular in England until recent times. There were four other saints, the most recently canonised was David Lewis (1616–1667) a Jesuit priest, who was executed at Usk for celebrating the Mass, when to do so, was punishable by death.

(a) 29 September, (b) 1 March

Declan

The English form of the Irish name 'Deaglan' of uncertain meaning. St Declan was the fifth-century disciple of St Colman, who became bishop in the district of Ardmore, Ireland. The name has become popular in modern Ireland.

24 July

Dennis *(Denys or Denis)*

From the Latin 'Dionysius' which originates from the Greek and referred to a devotee of the Greek god, Dionysos. The name was very popular in the early centuries of Christianity; there being over twenty saints, mostly martyrs, of this name. Its popularity in Europe, particularly in France, derives from the third-century missionary to the Gauls, who was martyred near Paris in 272 and was later adopted as patron of France. Commonly found in Britain (there are forty-one churches dedicated to the saint) up to the seventeenth century, when it dropped out of vogue; it returned to popular usage at the beginning of the twentieth century but not often found in the twenty-first.

9 October

Dominic

A truly European name, originating from the Latin 'dominicus' meaning 'belonging to the Lord'; it is found in a variety of forms ('Dominique' French; 'Domingo' Spanish; 'Domenico' Italian). Originally the name may have been given to children born on a Sunday (*dies dominica*). It appears as a Christian name in the thirteenth century in honour of St Dominic (a) (1170–1221) founder of the Order of Preachers (Dominicans) which exerted a powerful influence throughout Europe. However there were four saints of this name prior to the thirteenth century and eleven after, the most famous of the latter being St Dominic Savio (b) (1842–1857), the youngest non-martyr saint in history. Never commonly found in Britain before the Reformation, after, it was almost exclusively used in the Catholic community. In recent years it have gained more general usage.

(a) 8 August, (b) 8 March

Donald

From the Gaelic 'Donhnall' meaning 'ruler of the world'; it was originally a Scottish name associated with the MacDonald clan, the medieval Lords of the Isles. There was an eighth-century Scottish St Donald, who lived at Ogilivy in Forfarshire.

15 July

Dunstan

Meaning 'dark stone' from the Old English, this was the name of the great saintly Archbishop of Canterbury (909–988) who was much revered in the Middle Ages. He was adviser to kings, a noted musician and a skilled metalworker; this latter is particularly commemorated at Mayfield, Sussex, where he once had a residence. He is the patron of metalworkers and locksmiths. The name went out of use because of the Protestant Reformation, but was revived in the nineteenth century.

19 May

E

Eamon
The Gaelic form of 'Edmund' *(see Edmund)*.

Ebenezer
From the Hebrew, meaning 'stone of help'. The word appears in the Bible as the name of the stone raised by Samuel (1 Samuel 7:12) to commemorate the defeat of the Philistines. Introduced as a personal name by the seventeenth-century Puritans; it is still used in the USA.

Eden
Used for males and females, it appears to have originated from the Hebrew word, from Genesis 2:8, the Garden of 'delight'. Mainly found in the USA.

Edgar
An Old English name 'Eadgar', meaning 'wealthy spearman'. It was used in the royal house of Wessex at the time of King Alfred, and survived the Norman Conquest. St Edgar the Peaceful (d.975) was the English king who had St Dunstan as his adviser. Not in use from the thirteenth to nineteenth century when it was revived by the Romantics.

8 July

Edmond
The French form of Edmund *(see Edmund)*.

Edmund

Meaning 'rich guardian' from the Old English 'Eadmund'. There were two English kings (in addition to the martyr-king) of this name and several noteworthy saints. King Edmund (849–869), King of the East Angles, killed for his faith by invading Danes in Suffolk (a). St Edmund Rich (1180–1242) illustrious scholar and Archbishop of Canterbury (b). There were also three priests who were hung, drawn and quartered during the Elizabethan persecution of the Catholic Church; Edmund Arrowsmith, Edmund Campion, and Edmund Gennings. All honoured as saints.

(a) 20 November, (b) 20 November

Edward

From the Old English 'Eadweard' meaning 'prosperous ruler'; it is one of the few names popular throughout Europe for hundreds of years that originated from England. It is the name of three Anglo-Saxon kings and eight since the Norman Conquest. It is the influence of the Anglo-Saxons that established the name as a popular Christian name; Edward the Elder, son of Alfred the Great (d.924); St Edward the Martyr (d.979), and the famous St Edward the Confessor (d.1066), considered the model king; he also built Westminster Abbey. The popularity of the name in Elizabethan times is attested to by the fact that twelve of the Catholic martyrs of the period were named Edward.

(Edward the Confessor) 13 October

Edwin

Meaning 'prosperous friend' from the Old English 'Eadwine'. It was borne by the first Christian king of Northumbria; when he fell in battle (633) against the pagan Mercians, he was hailed and venerated as a martyr. Out of use for centuries, it was revived as a given name in the nineteenth century.

12 October

Eli

Hebrew name meaning 'height'; it was borne by the high priest who brought up the prophet, Samuel (1 Samuel 1–4). It was adopted and used by the seventeenth century Puritans, and is still occasionally found in the USA.

Elias

The Greek form of the Hebrew name 'Elijah' *(see Elijah)*.

Elijah

Hebrew name from the Bible meaning 'Yahweh (Lord) is God'. It was the name of the great prophet of the Old Testament whose eventful life can be found in 1 and 2 Kings. It was one of the most popular Old Testament names used in the Middle Ages; the following are derived from it; 'Ellis', 'Elie' (French), 'Elley', 'Elliot(t)' and 'Eliot'.

20 July

Eliot *(Elliott)* *(See Elijah).*

Elvis *(See Elwyn).*

Elwyn *(Elwin, Elvis)*

Of Celtic origin, the name means 'friend of the elves', but its origin is uncertain. There was one obscure Irish saint of the sixth century called St Elvis.

22 February

Emmanuel *(Emanuel)*

The New Testament Greek variant of the Hebrew word 'Immanuel' meaning 'God with us'; a title for the Messiah found in Isaiah 7:14 and applied to Jesus of Nazareth, the Christ, by Matthew 1:23. It found popularity in Latin countries as 'Manuel' or 'Manoel', but the name has not been much used in the English-speaking world. Three little-known saints bore the name.

(various including) 31 July

Enda

The English version of the Celtic name 'Eanna' meaning 'bird-like'. St Enda was, in the sixth century, the earliest organiser of Irish monasticism. He founded monasteries in the Boyne Valley, and finally settled on Inishmore, the largest of the Aran Islands.

21 March

Enoch

Hebrew name which possibly means 'dedicated' or 'skilled'. There were two biblical characters of this name: the son of Cain (Genesis 4:16) and the father of Methuselah (Genesis 5:21). There is an apocryphal book of the Bible attributed to him (see Jude 14). There was an obscure Scottish saint (d.1007) of this name.

25 March

Ephraim

It is the name of the second son of Joseph (see Genesis 41:52); a Hebrew name probably meaning 'fruitful'. There was a St Ephraem the Syrian (d.373) who wrote biblical commentaries. Still used in the Jewish community; since the eighteenth century it has been used occasionally in the USA.

9 June

Erasmus

From the Greek for 'beloved' or 'desired'. St Erasmus (d.303) was a bishop, who was martyred during the time of the Emperor Diocletian; very popular name in the late Middle Ages, and accepted as patron of sailors. The name is better known from the famous Dutch humanist scholar, Desiderius Erasmus (1465–1536). It has not proved popular in modern times.

2 June

Eric

Scandinavian name from the Old Norse meaning 'powerful ruler'. There was a St Eric, king of Sweden (d.1160), who attempted to establish a Christian kingdom and was murdered for his faith. Introduced into Britain by the Danes, the name dropped out of use but was reintroduced in the mid-nineteenth century.

18 May

Ethan

A Hebrew name meaning 'steadfast and firm', borne by two little-known people in the Bible (e.g. 1 Kings 4:31). Introduced into the USA by the Puritans, the name, in recent times has begun to be used again.

Eugene

The Old French form of the Greek name 'Eugenios' meaning 'nobly born'. A very popular name in the early years of the Christian Church; there are fourteen saints and four popes. Infrequently found in Britain in modern times, it is still popular in the USA, where it is sometimes shortened to 'Gene'.

13 November

Eustace

Originating from the Greek meaning 'fruitful', the name was borne by eight Christian saints; the most recent being the Lincolnshire priest, St Eustace White, a Roman Catholic martyr in Elizabethan times.

10 December

Ezekiel

Hebrew name meaning 'may God strengthen'; it was the name of one of the three major prophets, who prophesied among the Israelites in captivity in Babylon. The name was adopted and popular among the Puritans of seventeenth-century England and taken by them to the USA, where it continues to be used.

10 April

Ezra

Hebrew name meaning 'the one who helps'; it belonged to the Old Testament scribe (fifth–fourth century BC) to whom a book of the Bible is credited. First used in England in the seventeenth century by the Puritans (who rejected the traditional names of saints), it is still used in the USA and parts of Africa.

13 July

F

Fabian

The names of two early Christian saints, one a pope, it comes from the Latin name 'Fabianus'; its meaning is not clear but it could mean 'prosperous farmer'. It was introduced into England by the Normans but it has never been widely used.

20 January

Felix

From the Latin 'felix' meaning 'happy' or 'fortunate'; it appears in the New Testament (Acts 23–24) and it was one of the most popular names among the early Christians. There are at least seventy-four saints in the Christian calendar, and four popes, most of whom died as martyrs for their faith in second–fourth centuries. It was a popular name in Britain due to the high-standing of St Felix of Dunwich (d.647), who preached Christianity to the East Angles; the town of Felixstowe was named after him.

8 March

Ferdinand

Although of Germanic origin, meaning 'bold adventurer', it became very popular in Spain, where it was used by the kings of Castile. In the sixteenth century the Italian version, 'Ferdinando' became popular in England. There are two Spanish saints of this name, one of whom was Ferdinand III, King of Castille (1198–1252).

30 May

Fergus

An Old Irish name meaning 'the best choice'. There was a St Fergus of Scotland (d.721) an Irish bishop who worked in Perthshire, and it was the name of the grandfather of the great St Columba. Its main use is still found in Ireland and Scotland.

27 November

Finbar

The English form of the Gaelic 'Fionnbarr', meaning 'white-head'. There are two Irish saints of this name, both of the sixth century. The better known was the first bishop of Cork. The name is more often found in families of Irish descent.

4 July

Finian *(Finnian)*

Irish name derived from *'finnen'* meaning 'white' or 'fair'. Four Irish saints, abbots and bishops of the sixth and seventh centuries bore this name. The greatest of these was Finian of Clonard, (an important school of the period) who taught St Columba and other prominient figures of the time. Still in use in the Irish community.

12 December

Foster

The Old English form of the name 'Vedast'. There was a sixth-century saint of this name who was a co-worker of St Remigius in the conversion of the Franks. His memory is perpetuated in England by a church dedicated to him close to St Paul's in London, and several other pre-Reformation churches.

6 February

Francis

This is the English form of the Italian name 'Francesco', originally meaning 'French' of 'Frenchman'. There are twenty-two saints, all of whom were named after the famous St Francis of Assisi. His real name was 'Giovanni', but he was nicknamed 'Francesco', because his wealthy father had business connections with the French. A pleasure-seeking youth, Francis (1181–1226) turned his back on wealth and privilege to lead a life of dedicated poverty and humble service of the poor. So many young men were inspired by his example that in 1209 he founded the Order of Friars Minor; of whom there were 5000 by 1219. He sent his Friars to preach throughout Europe and especially into the university centres, including Oxford. In September 1224, Francis received a direct vision of Christ and the stigmata of Christ's Passion. He is best remembered for his love of nature, animals and gentle humility. His name has had unbroken popularity throughout the centuries in Europe and beyond.

4 October

Frank

Since the sixteenth century this has been the common abbreviation of Francis; however, it could also be a name in its own right deriving from the Germanic word that referred to a member of the tribe of the Franks, from which the country, once called Gaul, received the name France.

Fred

Short form of 'Frederick' *(see Frederick)*.

Frederick

A popular European name ('Fredericus' Latin; 'Friedrich' German; 'Federigo' Italian) it is of Germanic origin and means 'peaceful ruler'. There were two little-known saintly medieval bishops of this name. Once used by the Normans, it was reintroduced into Britain during Victorian times.

27 May

G

Gabriel

Hebrew name meaning 'man of God'; the biblical name of the messenger from God, the archangel who appeared to Daniel (Daniel 8:16), Zechariah (Luke 1:19) and, most famously, to Mary of Nazareth, the mother of Jesus (Luke 1:26). Three little-known saints took the name but it has only rarely been used in the English-speaking world.

29 September

Geoff

Short form of 'Geoffrey'.

Geoffrey *(Jeffrey)*

The modern name, from the Middle English 'Geffrey', originates from two Old Germanic names meaning 'God's divine peace'. Very popular in medieval England (e.g. Geoffrey Chaucer), it dropped out of favour from the fifteenth to the nineteenth centuries, but returned to usage in the twentieth century. There were several little-known medieval saints of this name.

25 September

George

One of the most European of names ('Georgius' Latin; 'Giorgio' Italian; 'Georg' Danish; 'Yuri' Russian) it originates from the Greek word for 'farmer' and came into English via Old French and Latin. There are ten saints of this name, but the most famous is the shadowy patron saint of England who was a Roman soldier and Christian martyr (d.c.300) who suffered during the reign of the Emperor Diocletian at Lydda, Palestine. All other legends, including the dragon story, have been shown to be fictitious. The Crusaders brought veneration of this soldier-saint back to Europe where the name has remained popular.

23 April

Gerald

From the Old German 'Gairovald' meaning 'spear-ruler'. It was introduced into England, and subsequently Ireland, by the Normans. Although its usage died out in England, it continued to be popular in Ireland. It was reintroduced into England during the nineteenth century. There were seven little-known medieval saints of this name.

5 April

Gerard

Probably introduced into England by the Normans, it is derived from an Old French name of Germanic origins meaning 'spear-brave'. More common in the Middle Ages than 'Gerald', there are sixteen saintly men who bore this name, the best known being the eighteenth century Gerald Majella who, as a tailor, joined the Redemptorist Order. He was famous for the many and varied supernatural phenomena which filled his life. Rarely used now, except in the Roman Catholic community.

16 October

Gervase *(Gervaise)*

A Norman name of no certain origin, the meaning is sometimes given as 'spear vassal'. The remains of two martyrs of the second century, Gervase and Protase, were discovered at Milan in 386; little else is known of them. Not common nowadays, it has occasional use among Catholic families.

19 June

Gideon

Hebrew name meaning 'destroyer' or 'he who cuts down'; biblical name of the sons of Joash (Judges 6:11) who led the Israelites against the Midianites. Adopted as a Christian name by the seventeenth-century Puritans and taken to the USA by the Pilgrim Fathers, where it is still in use.

1 September

Gilbert

From the Old German 'Gilsibert' meaning 'bright pledge'. Introduced into England by the Normans, it became one of the most popular Christian names. Of the three saints of this name, Gilbert of Sempringham (Lincolnshire) was the most famous; he founded the only English Religious Order of monks and nuns called the Gilbertine Order.

4 February

Giles

From the Latin and Greek original 'Aegidius' meaning 'young goat'. Very popular in the Latin form of 'Egidius' in the Middle Ages, there are over 160 churches in England dedicated to St Giles. There were several saints of this name, but the popular one was an eighth-century French abbot who was patron saint of cripples and beggars.

1 September

Godfrey

Meaning 'God's peace' the name comes from the Old German 'Godafrid'. The Normans introduced the name into Britain; it was one of the most popular names in the twelfth and thirteenth centuries. There were several little-known saints; Godfrey of Amiens (1066-1115) being specially regarded.

8 November

Gregory

From the Latin 'Gregorius' meaning 'the watchful or vigilant one'. The name has found its way into every European language because of its strong Christian past. A popular name in the early centuries of Christianity, there are at least twenty-four saints, including two great saintly theologians, Gregory of Nyssa (d.*c.*395) and Gregory Nazianzen (d.389) and the influential and renowned pope, St Gregory the Great (540–604).

3 September

Guy

The English form, via the French, of the Latin name 'Vitus' or 'Guido' meaning 'life' or 'the guide'. Several little-known medieval saints bore the name. It was introduced into Britain by the Normans, and remained popular until the 'Guy Fawkes' historical incident. It came back into use in the nineteenth century.

H

Hadrian *(See Adrian).*

Harold

An Anglo-Saxon name from *'here'* and *'weald'*, meaning 'army commander'. Not commonly found in the Middle-Ages, although there was the rather obscure St Harold (d.1168) who was said to have been murdered at Gloucester. It was revived again in the nineteenth century.

25 March

Henry

One of the most popular of continental names, it originates from the Old German meaning 'lord' or 'ruler of the estate'. Up until the seventeenth century, the English version ('Heinrich' German; 'Henri' French; 'Enrico' Italian) was 'Harry' or 'Herry'. The first St Henry (there are five saints of this name) was Henry the Good (973–1024) the Holy Roman Emperor, who gave protection to the Church in turbulant times.

13 July

Herbert

From the Old German 'Hariberet' meaning 'brilliant warrior'. Popular in Norman times it went out of use in the Middle Ages but was reintroduced in the nineteenth century. There are three little-known saints who bore this name.

20 August

Hilary

An ancient masculine name that is now more often given to girls. It originates from the Latin *'hilarius'* meaning 'cheerful'. The name was popular in the Middle-Ages (particularly in France) bestowed in honour of the great theologian, St Hilary of Poitiers (315–368); there are twelve other male saints, including one pope (d.468).

13 January

Hiram

A biblical name (see 2 Samuel 5:11) which is either Hebrew or Phoenician in origin, meaning 'most noble one'. Used by the seventeenth-century Puritans who took it to the USA. It soon dropped out of use in England but is still to be found in the USA.

Hubert

From the Old German 'Hugubert' meaning 'bright mind'. It was introduced into Britain by the Normans and it remained popular, probably because of medieval devotion to St Herbert, patron saint of hunters (d.727). According to a late legend he was converted to Christianity while out hunting.

3 November

Hugh

Of uncertain origin, it is probably from the French 'Hugues' meaning 'bright heart or spirit'. Introduced into England by the Normans, it was popular in medieval England because of a national veneration of

St Hugh of Lincoln (1135–1200). There are a further six European saints of this name, the most important being Hugh the Great of Cluny (1024–1109) who ruled over 1000 monasteries throughout Europe.

29 April

Hugo

Latin form of 'Hugh' *(see Hugh)*.

Humphrey

There was an Old English 'Hunfrith', but this appears to have been absorbed into the Norman name of Germanic origin, 'Hunfrid', meaning 'protector of the peace'. There were two little-known saints of this name. A popular name in medieval England, it is associated in modern times with celebrities like Humphrey Bogart and Humphrey Lyttelton.

8 March

I

Ignatius

A Latin name derived from the Roman family called 'Egnatius' probably meaning 'fiery patriot'. Christian use derives from the famous St Ignatius of Antioch (d.c.107) whose letters, learning and heroic death in the Roman arena inspired many (a). The name was most popular in Russia and Spain, and there were several Spanish saints, the most influential and important being the founder of the Society of Jesus (known as Jesuits) St Ignatius of Loyola (1491–1556) (b). In the English speaking world it is used mainly by Roman Catholics.

(a) 17 October, (b) 31 July

Immanuel *(See Emmanuel).*

Inigo

The Spanish version of 'Ignatius' *(see Ignatius).*

Ira

From the Hebrew meaning 'watchful'. This is the name of two biblical characters (see 2 Samuel 20:26; 23:26). Apart from the English Puritans of the seventeenth century, it has not been used in Britain but is still found in the USA.

Isaac

A Hebrew name meaning 'He (God) may laugh' (Genesis 17:19). Isaac was the child promised to Abraham and Sarah and honoured by Jews and Christians as one of the founding patriachs of the Chosen People. There are eight saints, mostly of the early years of Christianity. It is still used occasionally among Christian Jewish people (Messianic Jews) but has otherwise dropped out of use.

9 September

Isidore

From the Greek meaning 'the gift of Isis'. In spite of its pagan origins the name was very popular in the early centuries of Christianity. There are ten saints of this name in the Christian calendar, the most important being the great writer St Isidore of Seville (*c.*560–636). Outside of Spain it is regarded as a typically Jewish name and seldom used today.

4 April

Ivan

The Russian form of 'John' (*see John*).

Ivor (Ivar)

This probably originates from the Old Norse name 'Ivarr', meaning 'battle archer'; it was borne by several Danish kings of Dublin in the ninth century. It was also the name of a saint who was a contemporary of St Patrick.

23 April

J

Jack

Originally a pet form of the name 'John'; it is now a given name in its own right. It was, at one time, thought to have originated from the French 'Jacques' or the English 'James'; more recent research has shown that this is not the case *(see John)*.

Jacob

The English version of a Hebrew name which has uncertain origins and meaning. It is usually said to mean 'the heel grabber' or 'supplanter' (Genesis 25:26) but this is uncertain. It is the name of one of the greatest figures in the Old Testament, the patriarch who had twelve sons, who gave their names to the twelve tribes of Israel. Two of Christ's apostles bore this name. ('James' is an English form of the Hebrew name). The English translators of the New Testament used this latter translation but retained 'Jacob' for the Old Testament patriach. There is a St Jacob of Nisibis, a bishop of the fourth century.

15 July

James

The English form of the Latin 'Jacomus' a variant of 'Jacobus'; the name borne by two of Christ's apostles and the patriarch Jacob of Genesis *(see Jacob)*. This is a very European name, found in every European country; ('Jacques', France; 'Giacomo', Italy). It has remained popular throughout the ages; there are seventeen saints of this name and many blessed martyrs. St James the Greater (Apostle) was the son of Zebedee, brother of John (a). St James the Less was related to Jesus, either as cousin or, as some believe, brother. He was the leader of the Christian community (first bishop) of Jerusalem after Christ's Resurrection (b).

(a) 25 July, (b) 3 May

Jared

A Hebrew name meaning 'the descendant' found in the Bible where he is described as the father of Enoch (Genesis 5:18). Used by the Puritans of the seventeenth century, it enjoyed a brief revival in Britain in the 1960s.

Jason

From the Greek meaning 'the healer'; it was borne by the famous figure of Greek mythology, who led the Argonauts. The Christian use originates from the Jason mentioned in the Acts of the Apostles (17:5–9) who later, according to the Greek Church, converted the island of Corfu to Christianity.

12 July

Jasper *(Gaspar, Caspar)*

The English form of the name 'Gaspar', which is of Persian origin, meaning 'treasurer'. It was given, by tradition, to one of the Magi, or wise men, who visited the child Jesus. The gospel of Matthew does not specify how many Magi there were or their names. These were added by a later tradition, well established by the eleventh century. The name was first used in Britain in the fourteenth century.

Jed

Originally the shortened form of 'Jedidiah' a biblical name and alternative name for King Solomon (2 Samuel 12:25). It is now an accepted name in its own right; from the Hebrew meaning 'friend of God'. Still popular in the USA, the full name was frequently used by the seventeenth-century Puritans in both England and the USA.

Jeff

Shortened form of 'Jeffrey', now used independently *(see Jeffrey)*.

Jeffrey *(See Geoffrey)*.

Jeremiah

From the Hebrew meaning 'exalted by the Lord'; the name of one of the great biblical prophets of seventh–sixth century BC. His life and prophecies are found in the book of Jeremiah. It was much used by seventeenth-century Puritans and has returned to popularity in modern times; sometimes in the English form of 'Jeremy' *(see Jeremy)*.

1 May

Jeremy

The English form of 'Jeremiah' *(see Jeremiah)*.

Jerome

The English version, from the Greek of 'Hieronymos' meaning 'holy name'. There were several saints of this name, by far the most important being St Jerome (*c*.341–420) who was variously a secretary to a pope, a hermit living at Bethlehem and a famous Scripture scholar and translator of the Bible, who translated almost the whole Bible into Latin (called 'The Vulgate' text).

30 September

Jesse

This was the name of the father of King David (1 Samuel 16); it is from the Hebrew meaning either 'God exists' or 'God's gift'. Rarely used in modern times (except on occasion as a girl's name). From the popular use by the Puritans in the seventeenth century, it is still found in the USA.

Jethro

From the Hebrew meaning 'abundance' or 'excellence'. It was the name of Moses' father-in-law, who was a priest of the Kenites (Exodus 4:18). Popular among the seventeenth-century Puritans, it dropped out of use until there was a revival of interest in the 1970s.

Joachim

A Biblical name that probably comes from the Hebrew, 'Johoiachin' (2 Kings 24:8) meaning 'judgement of the Lord'. It was popular in medieval times, and there are several lesser-known saints bearing the name, because of the tradition that this was the name of the father of Mary, the mother of Jesus. This tradition is unreliable, as it rests only on the apocryphal gospel of James.

26 July

Joel

A common name in the Bible borne by thirteen different figures, the most important being one of the twelve minor prophets. Of Hebrew origin, it means 'Yahweh (the Lord) is God'. Always popular in the Jewish community, it is also used widely in the USA; there is a revival of interest in twenty-first century Britain.

13 July

John

This is the most perennially popular of names throughout Europe ('Jean' French; 'Hans' German; 'Giovanni' Italian; 'Juan' Spanish). From the Hebrew meaning 'God is gracious', it was the name of the cousin of Jesus, John the Baptist, and his beloved disciple, who is credited with the fourth gospel. Christian history is littered with famous figures bearing this name including 312 saints and twenty-three popes. Great theologians, e.g. John Chrysostom (347–407); influential mystics, e.g. St John of the Cross (1542–1591); famous martyrs, e.g. St John Fisher (1469–1535) all bore this popular name.

(St John, evangelist) 27 December

Johnathan *(See Jonathan).*

Johnny

Form of 'John' *(see John).*

Jolyon

Variant form of 'Julian' used in the Middle Ages *(see Julian).*

Jonathan

A popular biblical name, the most famous bearer being the brave and attractive son of King Saul (1 Samuel 14). From the Hebrew 'gift of God', it was not commonly used by Christians in Europe until after the Reformation.

Jordan

From the Hebrew name for the principal river of the Holy Land, meaning 'flowing down'. It appears to have an earlier root origin in the Old German 'Jordanes', but crusaders and pilgrims used bottled water from the River Jordan (where Christ was baptised) and often named their children after the river. Several medieval holy men, preachers and monks, bore the name.

(Blessed Jordan of Saxony) 15 February

Joseph

From the Hebrew meaning 'may God add' or 'God shall add'. A very popular name in Palestine at the time of Christ, from the Old Testament; the favourite son of Jacob (Genesis 37); Joseph of Arimathea who took the body of Jesus down from the cross and buried it; the husband of Mary, foster father of Jesus (Matthew 1:20). Hence, it was a popular name appearing throughout history in all European countries, and there have been twenty-seven saints bearing the name.

(St Joseph, husband of Mary) 19 March.

Josh

The short form of 'Joshua' (*see Joshua*).

Joshua

A Biblical name from the Hebrew, meaning 'saviour' or 'God is salvation'. He was the leader of the Israelites after the death of Moses, who led them into the Promised Land (The Book of Joshua). The most famous bearer of this name, we know by the Greek version, 'Jesus'.

'Joshua' was introduced into England as a Christian name after the Reformation. In Spain and South America, 'Jesus' has been frequently used, but not in the rest of Europe.

Josiah

The Greek version, 'Josias' is sometimes used. The original is Hebrew, meaning 'God heals'. There were two biblical characters (2 Kings 22; Zechariah 6:10) but the most famous English personage was the potter Josiah Wedgewood (1730–1795). Popular with the eighteenth-century Dissenters, it was always more popular in the USA than in Britain.

Judd

This began as a familiar form of 'Jordan' (*see Jordan*) in the Middle Ages but has become a name in its own right.

Jude

Derives from the Hebrew name 'Judah', the name of the fourth son of Jacob and Leah. Its meaning is not clear, some have suggested 'God leads'. Jude is also a variant of 'Judas'. Because of its link with Judas Iscariot, who betrayed Jesus, it has, until recently rarely been used as a Christian name. The only St Jude (patron of difficult or hopeless cases) was Judas Thaddaeus, another of Christ's apostles.

28 October

Julian

A very popular name among the Christians of the first centuries of Christianity, there are thirty saints, mostly martyrs. It is derived from the Latin 'Julianus'. In the late Middle Ages the name was used for both genders and the most famous English bearer of the name is the woman mystic Julian of Norwich (c.1342–1413).

(St Julian, patron of travellers) 13 February

Julius

Believed to be Greek, but its meaning is uncertain. Adopted as a Roman family name, it was used extensively by the early Christians; there being eight martyred saints during the first three centuries, three popes and a famous theologian and writer, Julius Africanus (c.160–240). There is a French version 'Jules', and the Welsh 'Iolo' is sometimes found.

(St Julius I, Pope) 12 April

Justin

A derivative of the Latin '*justus*' meaning 'the just one'; the English form of the name 'Justinus'. There are seven saints with this name, the most important being Justin Martyr (c.100–165) who argued and wrote to defend the Christian faith; he was beheaded in Rome.

1 June

Justus *(See Justin)*

Another name popular with the early Christians, there are fourteen saints in the Christian calendar. St Justus (d.627) was the third Archbishop of Canterbury a Benedictine monk who came to England from Rome with St Augustine.

10 November

Kane

From the Irish; it is the English form of the Celtic 'Cathan' meaning 'little warlike one'. There was an obscure Irish saint named St Cathan (sixth century), a bishop in Northern Ireland.

17 May

Karl *(See Carl)*.

Kean *(Keane)*

The English form of the Celtic name 'Cian' meaning 'bold' and 'handsome'. There was a sixth-century Welsh hermit-saint of this name.

11 December

Keenan

A variant of 'Kian' (*see Kean*).

Ken

Short form of 'Kenneth' (*see Kenneth*).

Kenneth

Of Gaelic origin, meaning 'the handsome'. There are two little-known saints of this name; the more prominent being a Welsh hermit of the sixth century, who lived on the peninsula of Gower.

1 August

Kenny
>The familiar form of 'Kenneth', but also a name in its own right. There is a St Kenny who was a sixth-century Irish missionary to Scotland. The town Kilkenny is named after him.
>
>*11 October*

Kevin
>From the Irish 'Coemgen' meaning 'comely' or 'gentle'. St Keven (d.c.618) was the abbot-founder of the famous Glendalough monastery and in modern times, one of the patrons of Dublin.
>
>*3 June*

Kieran *(Kieron)*
>The English form of the Gaelic 'Cieran' which means 'small and dark-skinned'. There are two sixth-century Irish saints of this name; Bishop Kieran has been called 'the first-born of the saints of Ireland'; he was ordained Bishop of Ossory by St Patrick. The other saint was the abbot-founder of a monastery at West Meath.
>
>*(St Kieran, bishop) 5 March.*

Killian *(Kilian)*
>From the Gaelic 'Cillian' meaning 'little warlike one'. Three Irish saints of the seventh century share this name; the most famous was a missionary and Bishop of Wurzburg, where he is still honoured.
>
>*8 July*

Kristen
>This is the Danish form of 'Christian' *(see Christian)*.

L

Ladislas

A Hungarian name of uncertain origins; it was borne by the great Hungarian saint-king (1040–1095) who was a national hero (known in Hungary as Laszlo). Also borne by two other East European saints. Found mainly among Polish or East European Christians.

27 June

Lambert

From the Old German 'Landebert' meaning 'bright land' or 'rich land'. Brought to England from the twelfth century onwards by Flemish weavers, among whom it was popular because of St Lambert of Maestricht (d.709), bishop and martyr. There are four other saints of the same name.

17 September

Laurence *(Lawrence)*

From the French form of the Latin 'Laurentius' meaning 'person from Laurentum'. This name was very popular in medieval England due to two influences; the popularity of St Laurence who was martyred in Rome in 258 (a) (there are 237 English churches dedicated to him) and St Laurence of Canterbury (d.619) a respected Archbishop of Canterbury (b). In Ireland the name has been widely used because of St Laurence O'Toole, a reforming bishop of the twelfth century (c). There have been nine other saints of this name.

(a) 10 August, (b) 2 February, (c) 14 November

Leander

This is the Latin form of the Greek name 'Leandros', meaning 'the lion man'. Apart from the Leander of Greek mythology, there was a famous Christian saint of the sixth century. He was a friend of St Gregory the Great and bishop of Seville, where he is still venerated.

27 February

Len

Short form of 'Leonard' *(see Leonard)*.

Leo

From the Greek word for 'lion' via the Latin *'leo'*. It has always been a popular Christian name being borne by fifteen saints and thirteen popes. The most famous pope being St Leo the Great (d.461). 'Leon' has been quite common in France and this spelling was popular in medieval England. It has remained popular in the Jewish community.

10 November

Leonard

From the Old German 'Leonhard' meaning 'lion brave'; it became a popular French name due to the influence of St Leonard of Noblac (d.559), whose cult was widespread in Western Europe. The Normans brought the name to England, and 177 English parish churches were dedicated to St Leonard (and one Sussex seaside town was named after him). The name enjoyed a revival in the nineteenth century.

6 November

Leopold

From the Old German 'Leudbald' meaning 'brave for the people'. There is a St Leopold the Good (1073–1136), but the use of the name in Britain, from the nineteenth century, was more likely because of the immense popularity of Leopold, King of the Belgians (1790–1865), an uncle of Queen Victoria.

15 November

Lewie

An alternative spelling of 'Louis' *(see Louis)*.

Lewis

The usual English form of the French name 'Louis' *(see Louis)*.

Lex

The short form of 'Alex' *(see Alexis and Alexander)*.

Liam

The Irish form of 'William' *(see William)*.

Linus

This is the Latin form of the Greek 'Linos' meaning 'flax-coloured hair'. There is a character in Greek mythology, but Christian usage comes from St Linus, the bishop of Rome that followed St Peter for the years 67–79 AD. In the 1960s, the cartoon character in the famous strip-cartoon, *'Peanuts'*, encouraged a revival of interest in the name.

23 September

Llewelyn

A popular Welsh name derived from the ancient name 'Llywelyn' meaning 'lion like'. There is a sixth-century Welsh saint, a monk at Welshpool, of this name.

7 April

Lorcan

The English form of a Gaelic name; it is also found in English as 'Laurence'. St Lorcan was Laurence O'Toole *(see Laurence)*.

Louis

Of Old Frankish origin, this very common French name is found throughout Europe ('Ludovicus' Latin; 'Luigi' Italian; 'Luis' Spanish; 'Ludwig' German; 'Lewis' English). Before the French Revolution it was the most popular male forename; eighteen French kings bore the name, one of whom, Louis IX (1214–1270), was revered as a saint. There were numerous other saints of this name. It was introduced into England soon after the Norman Conquest, in the form of 'Lewis', which gave rise to a number of surnames.

25 August

Lucas

Variant of 'Luke' used by the translators of the authorised version of the New Testament *(see Luke)*.

Luke

From the Latin 'Lucas', but originally a Greek word meaning 'a person from Lucania'. It is the name of the first-century Gentile doctor from Antioch who was a friend of St Paul, and the writer of the third gospel and the Acts of the Apostles (a). The name is not found in

Britain before the twelfth century but it has been in regular use since. There are eight other saints including the Englishman, Luke Kirby, who in the time of Elizabeth I (1582) was tortured in the Tower of London and executed for being a Catholic priest (b).

(a) 18 October, (b) 30 May

Luther

Taken from the surname of the famous theologian and reformer, Martin Luther (1483–1546); who should not be confused with the American civil rights leader, Martin Luther King. Of Old German origin the word means 'famous warrior'. Mostly found in the USA, especially after the assassination of Martin Luther King.

M

Magnus

From the Latin for 'great' and was first applied to the Emperor Charlemagne (Carolus Magnus or Charles the Great). It was adopted by the Scandinavians and there were seven Norwegian kings of this name. There are eleven little-known saints who also bore the name.

(St Magnus of the Orkneys) 16 April

Malachy (Malachi)

The English form of the Irish 'Maolmhaodhog'. The original Irish bearer of the name was an Irish king who defeated the Norse invaders. Later chroniclers linked this with the name of the Old Testament prophet, Malachi (Hebrew for 'my messenger'), the last of the twelve minor prophets. Later Christians were more likely named after the famous Irish saint, Malachy O'More (1094–1148) Archbishop of Armagh and energetic reforming churchman.

3 November

Malcolm

The English form of the Gaelic name 'Maol-Columb' meaning 'follower', or 'disciple of St Columba'. The name 'Columba' means 'dove' (*see Colum*), the sixth-century Irish saint who did much to convert the Scots. Hence, it has for centuries been a favourite Scottish name but more widely used in the twentieth century.

Manny

The familiar for the name 'Emmanuel'; used mainly in the Jewish community *(see Emmanuel)*.

Manuel

The Spanish and Portuguese form of 'Emmanuel' *(see Emmanuel)*.

Marc

The French form of 'Mark' but gaining in popularity in Britain *(see Mark)*.

Marcel

A French name taken from the Latin name 'Marcellus'. Very popular with the Christians of the first four hundred years of Christianity; there are seventeen saints, including one pope. The French connection is with St Marcellus (d.274), a Roman missionary to Gaul who was beheaded for his faith there.

29 June

Marcus

The original Latin form of the English 'Mark', a name of uncertain origins, perhaps from 'Mars' the Roman god of war; so the usual meaning given for the name is 'follower of Mars' *(see Mark)*.

Mark

From the Latin name 'Marcus' *(see Marcus)*. It was borne by the writer of the second gospel, although scholars believe that Mark was the first to write an account of the 'Good News' (gospel). He has traditionally been identified with John Mark, the cousin of Barnabas (Colossians 4:10). According to tradition, he founded the Christian community in Alexandria where he died a martyr. His body was transferred to Venice in the ninth century. There are twenty other saints of this name, including a pope. In spite of this, the name only became widely used in modern times.

25 April

Martin *(Martyn)*

The English form of the Latin name 'Martinus' probably derived from the Roman god of war, Mars; so the name is believed to mean 'warlike' or 'warrior'. This was a very popular name throughout Europe in the Middle Ages and since, due first to the fame of St Martin of Tours (a) (*c*.316–397) and later, for Protestants, the influence of the reformer, Martin Luther (1483–1546). Added to both of these, in modern times, there is the popularity of the pastor and civil rights leader, Martin Luther King (1929–1968). Besides numerous saints (another popular one being St Martin Porres, 1569–1639) (b) there have been five popes.

(a) 11 November, (b) 3 November

Marty

Short form of 'Martin'; but it has been used as a name in its own right.

Matthew *(Mathew)*

From the Hebrew 'Mattathiah' meaning 'gift of God'. It became 'Matthaeus' or 'Matthias' in Latin. It was introduced into England by the Normans and was very common in the Middle Ages. Hence, there are several saints of this name, but the most famous was the evangelist, author of the first gospel. He was also known as Levi and was originally a tax-collector before becoming one of Christ's twelve apostles.

21 September

Matthias

A form of 'Matthew' *(see Matthew)*. To distinguish the two apostles of the same name (one was chosen to replace Judas to make the number up to twelve (see Acts 1:23) the translators of the New Testament spelt the second one this way. Details of his later life are not known.

14 May

Maurice

From the Latin name 'Mauricius', derived from 'Maurus' meaning 'Moorish-looking' or 'swarthy'. This was the name of the Roman officer and member of the famed Theban military unit, who, as a Christian, refused to worship the emperor as a god and offer incense to the Roman gods (*c*.287). The whole unit followed his example and were massacred *en masse* by other, pagan, legions near Agaumun, Switzerland. The name was introduced into England by the Normans, and sometimes appears in the form of 'Morris' *(see Morris)*.

22 September

Max

Short form of 'Maximilian' *(see Maximilian)*.

Maximilian

This originates from the combination of two Latin words – 'Maximus' (the greatest) and 'Aemilianus' which was the family name of the writer, Scipio; so, combined, it was a form of flattery. Borne by three martyrs of the third century, it became famous in the twentieth century because of St Maximilian Kolbe (1894–1941) who rescued Jews in Cracow, Poland, and died heroically for another prisoner in Auschwitz concentration camp. He is commemorated in stone above the west door of Westminster Abbey, London. For historical reasons, the name has been particularly popular in Germany.

14 August

Micah

Hebrew name from 'Micaiah' meaning 'who is like God?' It is the name of one of the minor prophet, and a book of the Bible. Not often found in Britain but occasionally used in the USA.

15 January

Michael

The English form of a Hebrew name that comes from the same root as 'Micah' meaning 'who is like God?' The Bible describes the role of the Archangel Michael (Daniel 10:13 and Revelation 12:7) as captain of the heavenly host of angels, so he has been the patron of soldiers. Popular name throughout Europe, there are 687 churches in England dedicated to him; there are eight lesser-known saints.

29 September

Mick
Short form of 'Michael' (*see Michael*).

Mihangel
Old Welsh form of 'Michael' (*see Michael*).

Mike
Short form of 'Michael', sometimes used as an independent name *(see Michael)*.

Miles
Introduced into England by the Normans, its antecedents are not clear; it may have come from the Old German 'Milo'. This form of the name was common in the Middle-Ages. It could mean 'millstone' from the Greek; or 'soldier' from the Latin. Several saintly persons bore the name Milo, and a Catholic martyr, Miles Gerard, died at Rochester in 1590.

30 April

Milo
Alternative form of 'Miles' (*see Miles*).

Morris
A variant from of 'Maurice' *(see Maurice)* popular in England during the Middle Ages; however, it has developed into a forename in its own right in modern times.

Moses
The English form of the Hebrew name 'Moshe'; it is believed to be of Egyptian origin and said to mean 'taken from the water'; which would fit the story of Moses, the Jewish leader and patriarch, who first bore

the name (Exodus 2). Moses was the great leader and lawgiver who under God's direction, liberated the Hebrews from slavery in Egypt. Although it is now mainly used in the Jewish community, it was popular in early Christian times and among the seventeenth-century Puritans. Five early Christian martyrs bore the name.

4 September

Moss

Taken from the medieval form of 'Moses' *(see Moses)*.

Muirius

The Irish form of 'Maurice' *(see Maurice)*.

Mungo

From the Gaelic, meaning 'amiable'; it was an epithet applied to St Kentigern and was used occasionally as a Christian name in his native Scotland, especially in the Glasgow area.

13 January

Myron

From the Greek word *'myron'* meaning 'fragrant oil'. Used widely by the early Christians because of its association with one of the gifts brought by the Magi (three wise men) to the child Jesus (Matthew 2:11). There were two third-century saints, both venerated in the Eastern Church, where the name is more widely used than in the West.

17 August

N

Nahum

From the Hebrew meaning 'comforter'. It was the name of one of the minor prophets of the Old Testament, the Book of Nahum has only three chapters and comes after Micah. A popular Jewish name it was often used by the Dissenter Christians of the seventeenth century.

1 December

Nat

Short form of 'Nathan' (*see Nathan*).

Nathan

A Hebrew name meaning 'gift of God'. It was the name of an Old Testament prophet who had the courage to challenge King David's immoral behaviour. Six other lesser biblical figures had this name.

Nathaniel

This is a name from the New Testament, originally from the Hebrew meaning 'God has given'. It was borne by one of Christ's apostles, who is probably the same person as 'Bartholomew' (John 1:45). Not used in England before the Reformation, it was popular with the Puritans; still occasionally found.

24 August

Ned

Short form of 'Edward' (*see Edward*).

Nichol *(Nicol)*

Short form of 'Nicholas' that was widely used in the Middle Ages *(see 'Nicholas')*.

Nicholas *(Nicolas; Nickolas)*

From the Latin 'Nicolaus' which in turn comes from the Greek, meaning 'victorious leader'. The original St Nicholas (there are twelve saints including one pope) is one of the most popular saints of all time. His story is almost all legend, except the bare facts that he was Bishop of Myra, Lycia, and died about 350. Patron saint of sailors, pawnbrokers and children; he is also patron of Russia and Greece. His legends suggest great generosity and he has become 'Father Christmas' or 'Santa Claus', which is a corruption of his name (Sinter Claus) via the Dutch of New Amsterdam (New York). In some countries his feast day is celebrated as Christmas Day.

6 December

Nick

Short form of 'Nicholas' *(see Nicholas)*.

Ninian

Probably of Celtic origin, its meaning is uncertain. It was the name of a fifth-century saint (d.*c*.432), who preached Christianity to the Picts of the north of England; he is believed to have been a bishop. Used primarily in Scotland, the name has found wider use in the twenty-first century.

26 August

Noah

Uncertain in origin but believed to be Hebrew, meaning 'rest' or 'comfort' (but some suggest 'long-lived'). The story of the biblical character is familiar (see Genesis 6:9) as the good man chosen by God to save his family and representatives of the animal kingdom, to be the 'new creation' with a fresh start after the flood. The name has found occasional use since its popularity in seventeenth-century England and the USA.

Noel

The French form of *'natalis'* which is from the Latin *'natalis dies'* (meaning 'day of birth') referring to the birthday of Christ, Christmas. Two rather obscure saints bear the name, but it was more likely bestowed on a child who was born at Christmas time.

the Christmas period

Noll

The familiar form of 'Oliver' *(see Oliver)*.

Norbert

Of Germanic origin from the words *'nord'* (north) and *'berht'* (bright). There is only one St Norbert (c.1080–1134) who was a German prince who gave up fame and fortune to preach the gospel. He became the founder of the Norbertines or Premonstratensians (also known as the White Canons). Many monasteries were founded throughout Europe, especially in France, Hungary and Britain; famous for their work for religious revival in Europe after World War II. The name is more commonly found in the USA than in Britain.

6 June

O

Oliver
Originates from the French name 'Olivier' which appears to come from the Latin for 'olive tree'. It was fairly popular name in the Middle Ages due to association with the court of the Emperor Charlemagne. Popular in the Roman Catholic community in modern times because of St Oliver Plunket (1629–1681) the Irish bishop who died at Tyburn, London, for (the charge read) 'propagating the Catholic religion'.
11 July

Ollie
Familiar form of 'Oliver' *(see Oliver)*.

Omar
From the Hebrew meaning 'talkative'. Found in the Bible (Genesis 36:11) it was used occasionally in Puritan society, but in recent years it has become associated with the Islamic community.

Oran *(Oren)*
The English form of the Gaelic 'Olharan' meaning 'sallow'. There is an obscure Irish saint, St Oran of Meath (*c*.563). The 'Oren' form is found in the Bible in 1 Chronicles 2:25. Never much used in Britain, but it is found in USA.
22 October

Osmond *(Osmund)*

From the Old English meaning 'divine protector'. It was in general use in England before the Norman Conquest and taken up and used by the Normans. There was just the one St Osmund; he was appointed bishop of Salisbury in 1072 where he finished building the cathedral. The name is not much used in modern times.

4 December

Oswald

From the Old English 'Osweald' meaning 'divinely powerful'. There were two English saints of this name. The first was the seventh-century King of Northumbria (a); the second was an Archbishop of York (b) (d.922). Popular in the Middle Ages, the name dropped completely out of use, but has returned to occasional use in the twenty-first century.

(a) 5 August, (b) 28 February

Otto

The modern German form of 'Odo', which means 'wealthy, prosperous man'. There were two saints of this name, the better known is Otto of Bamberg (1062–1139) a German missionary and bishop.

2 July

Owen

A common Welsh name although its origin and meaning is uncertain. There are two, rather obscure, saints of this name; both lived in the seventh century.

4 March

P

Paddy

The familiar shortened form of 'Patrick' *(see Patrick)*.

Padraig

The Irish form of 'Patrick' *(see Patrick)*.

Patrick

From the Latin *'patricius'* meaning 'nobleman'. This was the name adopted by a Christian Briton, named Sucat, when he was consecrated as a missionary to Ireland, where he had previously been enslaved as a youth. St Patrick (*c.*390–461) established the Christian Church in Ireland. Many legends surround his life; however, he founded the See of Armagh and his hard work and sanctity earnt him the title 'Apostle of Ireland'. There are three more little-known saints in the Christian calendar of the same name.

17 March

Paul

From the Latin for 'small'. This is a widely used name in all Christian countries ('Paolo' Italian and Portuguese; 'Pablo' Spanish; 'Pavel' Russian). This was the name Saul of Tarsus took after his conversion experience on the road to Damascus (Acts 9) before his great missionary journeys. He endured many hardships and his thirteen letters to the communities he founded were accepted by the Church as inspired Scripture. Interestingly this name is more popular in England in modern times than it was throughout the whole of the Middle Ages. There have been thirty-nine saints named after the apostle to the Gentiles and six popes.

29 June

Peter

The Latin name 'Petrus' comes from the Greek 'Petros' which is a translation of the Aramaic 'Cephas' (demonstrating how Christ's teaching went from Aramaic to Greek and then into Latin) which means 'stone' or 'rock'. This was the nickname that Jesus gave to Simon Bar Jona, whom Christ chose as the leader of the twelve apostles and later became the first bishop of Rome. This has been one of the most popular male forenames in history; it is prominient in all European countries. In England there are 1140 churches dedicated to St Peter. The most common form in the Middle Ages was 'Piers'; at the Reformation the name dropped out of use because of its association with Rome and Catholicism. It returned to popularity in the more enlightened twentieth century. There are seventy-four other saints who were given the name of the leader of the apostles.

29 June

Phil

Short form of 'Philip' *(see Philip)*.

Philip

From the Greek meaning 'lover of horses'. As a Greek name it was popular in the Greek period of the Church. It appears four times in the Bible; in the New Testament it is the name of one of Christ's apostles who came from Bethsaida and died a martyr's death in Phrygia (a). It is also the name of one of the seven deacons chosen to help the apostles (b) (Acts 6:5; 8:26–40). It has been a popular name throughout the centuries (there are sixteen more saints) and throughout Europe. In England, St Philip Howard (d.1595) is honoured at Arundel, Sussex, for dying in defence of his Catholic faith in the Tower of London (c).

(a) 3 May, (b) 6 June, (c) 19 October

Phineas

From the Greek meaning 'mouth of brass'; it is found three times in the Old Testament, borne by minor characters, e.g. Aaron's grandson (Numbers 25:6–15). It was a popular name among the seventeenth-century Puritans and remains popular in some parts of the USA.

Piers

The medieval form of 'Peter' *(see Peter)*.

Quentin

From the Latin word for 'fifth'. The French town of St Quentin was named after a Roman missionary to northern France who was martyred there (*c.*287). The name was brought to England by the Normans.

31 October

Quitin *(Quinton)*

Variant forms of Quentin *(see Quentin)*.

Ralph

Originally from the Old Norse, via the Normans, the English name is more commonly found in its French form of 'Raoul', meaning 'wolf counsel'. A popular name in Tudor times, as 'Ralf'. There are several saints of that period, particularly St Ralph Sherwin (d.1581) and a ninth-century Benedictine saint.

21 June

Ray

The short form of 'Raymond' *(see Raymond)*.

Raymond *(Raymund)*

From the Old German 'Raginmund' meaning 'wise protection'. A very popular European name in the twelfth–fourteenth centuries, when the six saints of this name lived; the most famous being St Raymond of Penafort, a famous Spanish preacher. The Normans brought the name to England.

7 January

Reg

The short form of 'Reginald' *(see Reginald)*.

Reginald

From the Old English 'Regenweald', meaning 'mighty power'. Three saintly monks bore the name, although it is derived from Reynold *(see Reynold)*.

1 February

Reuben

A biblical name from the Hebrew meaning 'behold the son'. This was the name of one of Jacob's sons (Genesis 30:14) and the name of one of the twelve tribes of Israel. Steadily popular as a Jewish name, it enjoyed Christian usage in the seventeenth century and again in the nineteenth.

Reynold

The Old English 'Regenweald' meaning 'mighty power' combined, after the Norman Conquest, with the Old French 'Reinald' to produce a name which was popular in Norman England. There are no saints of this particular name.

Richard

An Old French name, derived from Frankish roots, meaning 'powerful one'; it was imported into England by the Normans. It has enjoyed continual popularity in Britain from the Norman Conquest to today. This included the folk hero, King Richard the Lionheart (1157–1199) but also the saintly bishop of Chichester, Richard de Wych (1197–1253), and the English mystic, Richard Rolle (1300–1349).

(St Richard of Chichester) 3 April

Richie

A familiar form of 'Richard' *(see Richard)*.

Ricky

A familiar form of 'Richard' *(see Richard)*.

Robert

A popular English name derived from the French meaning 'bright and shining fame' and imported by the Normans. (It was the name of William the Conqueror's father). There are nine medieval saints of this name, and the famous Jesuit intellectual St Robert Bellarmine (1542–1621). Many surnames and nicknames (e.g. 'Rob', 'Bob', 'Nob' and 'Robin') have been derived over the centuries from 'Robert'.

3 April

Roderick

Derived from the Old German 'Hrodic' meaning 'famous wealthy ruler'. Introduced into England by the Normans it did not survive the Middle Ages but was reintroduced in the nineteenth century. There is only one obscure saint of this name.

13 March

Roger

The name emerged from a blending of the Old English 'Hrothgar' and, at the Norman Conquest, the French 'Roger', meaning 'famous spearman'. It was a popular name throughout the Middle Ages and gave rise to many surnames. There are several saintly personages of this name, all rather obscure.

15 November

Ronald

Originally the Scottish equivalent of 'Reginald' meaning 'mighty power'. St Ronald (d.1158) was a chieftain of Orkney who built the cathedral of St Magnus at Kirkwall. He died a martyr's death.

20 August

Rowan

It is the English version of the Gaelic name 'Ruadhan', meaning 'little brown one'. It was borne by a little-known saint of the sixth century who founded the monastery at Lothra. (The name can be used by either gender).

S

St John
(Pronounced 'sin-jen'). Obviously a name originating from St John; either the gospel-writer or the baptist, cousin of Jesus. Mainly found in the Roman Catholic community.

24 June

Sam
Short form of 'Samuel' *(see Samuel)*.

Samson *(Sampson)*
From the Hebrew 'Shimshon' meaning 'sun child'. It was the name of the famous Jewish champion and judge (Judges 13–16). It was also the name of two sixth-century saints. The most well-known was the Abbot of Caldy Island who became one of the greatest missionaries of his period; he is still revered in Wales and Brittany.

28 July

Samuel
This is the English form of the Hebrew name 'Shemuel', probably meaning 'God has listened'. The name of one of the greatest of the Hebrew prophets (eleventh century BC) who anointed Saul as King; his story can be found in 1 and 2 Samuel (they are known as First and Second Kings in the Orthodox and Roman Catholic traditions).

Always popular in the Jewish community, the name entered widespread use in general society after the Reformation.

20 August

Seamas *(Seamus)*

The Irish form of 'James' *(see James)*.

Sean

The Irish form of 'John' *(see John)*.

Sebastian

From the Latin 'Sebastianus' meaning 'man from Sebaste'. It was the name of one of the most renowned of the Roman martyrs. According to unreliable sources, Sebastian was an officer in the imperial guard of Diocletian, when he converted to Christianity. Convicted, the Emperor handed him over to his fellow officers to fire their arrows at (*c*.288). His sufferings (arrows all over his body) have been a favourite subject for many artists over the centuries.

20 January

Seumas *(Seumus)*

Scottish Gaelic form of 'James' *(see James)*.

Shamus

The English spelling sometimes adopted for the Irish 'Seamus' *(see Seamus)*.

Shaun

The English spelling of the Irish 'Sean' *(see Sean)*.

Silas

A Greek name, a short form of 'Silouanus' meaning 'from the forest'. It was the name of St Paul's travelling companion (Acts 15:22; 18:5). Legend has it that he became the first bishop of Corinth. The name was not use in England before the Reformation.

13 July

Silvester *(Sylvester)*

From the Latin meaning 'woody' or 'growing in a wood'. There were five saints of this name, the most important being Pope Sylvester (d.335) who was the first pope to govern the Western Church free of Roman persecution.

31 December

Simeon

A biblical name, from the Hebrew 'Shimeon' meaning 'one who hears'. A common name in Israel, there are several biblical figures, particularly the elderly 'just and devout' Jew who blessed the child Jesus in the Temple (Luke 2:25). There are ten other saints of this name, mostly hermits; the most renowned being Simeon Stylites – there is an elder (390–459) and a younger (521–697). Both amazingly lived a hermit existence on top of a stone pillar.

5 January

Simon

This is the more usual English form of 'Simeon' *(see Simeon)*. There are seven saints of this name; apart from Simon who became 'Peter' *(see Peter)*. From an English point of view the most famous would be St Simon Stock (1165–1265) who was one of the first Englishmen to join the Order of Carmelites. He established the Order in England, particularly at Oxford (1253) and Cambridge (1248). Nowadays he is associated with the Carmelite Priory at Aylesford, Kent, where his relics are kept.

16 May

Stan

Short version of 'Stanislaus' or 'Stanley' *(see Stanislaus).*

Stanislaus

This is a Slavic name meaning 'stand for glory'. It was the name of two famous Polish saints; the first (1030–1079) was rather like Thomas Becket, murdered in church while at Mass for opposing the Polish king (a). The second Stanislaus Kostka (1550–1568) died as a young Jesuit priest (b). The name is popular in Polish circles, whether in Poland or in Britain.

(a) 11 April, (b) 13 November

Stephen *(Steven)*

This is the English variant of the Graeco-Latin name 'Stephanus' meaning 'the crowned one'. It is one of the most European of names ('Stefano' Italian; 'Etienne' French; 'Esteban' Spanish; 'Istvan' Hungarian) and one of the most popular of all male Christian names throughout the centuries. Its Christian usage springs from the deacon Stephen (Acts 6–7) who was the first Christian martyr. There have been over thirty further saints of the same name, including a saintly king of Hungary (c.935–1038) and a pope.

(St Stephen martyr) 26 December

T

Ted *(Teddy)*
Short form of 'Edward' *(see Edward)* or 'Theodore' *(see Theodore)*.

Terence
From the Latin name 'Terentius' which is of uncertain origin and meaning. There were several little known saints bearing this name in the early centuries of Christianity. Not often found, except in Ireland.

21 June

Theo
Short form of 'Theodore' *(see Theodore)*.

Theodore
From the Greek name 'Theodoros' meaning 'gift of God'. This was a very popular name in Christianity for the first thousand years of its history. There were twenty-nine saints, including early martyrs, an Archbishop of Canterbury (*c.*602–690) and St Theodore Studites (759–826) a famous monastic leader of the Eastern Orthodox Church.

(St Theodore of Canterbury) 19 September

Thomas
From an Aramaic word meaning 'twin'; in the gospels it is the name of one of the twelve apostles. It became – and has remained – one of the most popular of male names, perhaps because the doubts of the Apostle

Thomas made him seem human and approachable (a). There have been sixty saintly men of this name, including the great theologian Thomas Aquinas (b) (1225–1274); the martyred Archbishop of Canterbury (c), Thomas Becket (1118–1170); and the Chancellor of England who opposed King Henry VIII, Thomas More (d) (1478–1535). At the height of its popularity in Tudor times, the name was shortened to 'Thome', and later to 'Tom'. It was so popular in the twentieth century, that British soldiers in the World War I were nicknamed 'Tommies'.

(a) 3 July, (b) 28 January,
(c) 28 December, (d) 22 June

Timothy

This is the English form of the Greek name 'Timotheos' meaning 'honouring God'. It was the name of the Apostle Paul's convert who became a travelling companion, and to whom Paul addressed two letters found in the Bible (1 and 2 Timothy). Although there were eight early Christian saints of this name, it was not widely used in the English-speaking world until well after the Reformation.

26 January

Tobias

From the Hebrew 'Tobiah' meaning 'God is good'. It is the name of several biblical characters but particularly the hero of the deuterocanonical (not included in all bibles) Book of Tobit. The story told there, of Tobias and the angel, was very popular in the Middle Ages. There was also a fourth-century martyr of this name.

2 November

Tony
Shortened form of 'Antony' or 'Anthony' *(see Antony)*.

V

Valentine

Derived from *'valens'* meaning 'strong'. There were probably six saints of this name, all from the first centuries of Christianity, and all quite obscure. The martyr who is celebrated on 14 February had been a priest and a doctor and died for his faith at Rome in 269.

The custom of sending 'Valentines' on 14 February is based on a medieval belief that birds begin to pair on this day.

14 February

Vic

Short form of 'Victor' *(see Victor)*.

Victor

From the Latin word *'victor'* meaning 'conqueror' or 'winner'. A very popular name among the early Christians; there were over thirty saints, including the first African pope (d.198) and Victor III (1027–1087) who had been a successful Benedictine abbot of Monte Casino. Rarely found in the Middle Ages; the name was popular in France after the Revolution.

16 September

Vincent

Taken from the Latin name 'Vincentius' derived from *'vincens'* meaning 'conquering'. There are twenty-four saints who bore this name, two of whom are famous: Vincent de Paul (1581–1660) renowned for his care of the poor and disadvantaged, and founder of the Sisters of Charity (a); Vincent Ferrer (1350–1419) an illustrious preacher (b).

(a) 27 September, (b) 5 April

Virgil

This name is more frequently found in the USA than Britain. The original Latin name, meaning 'staff bearer', was 'Vergilius'. There was a renowned Latin poet of this name but the Christian usage came from three early martyr-saints and an Irish monk, abbot and missionary (d.784).

26 June

Vivian

This originates from the Latin name 'Vivianus' meaning 'the lively one'. There were three little-known saints of this name. In the Middle Ages the name was sometimes spelt 'Fithian'. Although originally a boy's name, it has become more frequently used for girls in modern times.

28 August

W

Walter

From the Old German word 'Waldhar' meaning 'mighty warrior'. The Normans introduced the name into England and it was very popular in medieval times. There have been five rather obsure saints with this name.

4 June

Wesley

Taken from the surname of the founder of Methodism, John Wesley (1703–1791), also his brother Charles Wesley (1707–1788) who was a great and prolific hymn writer. At first the name was only used in Methodist circles, but it is now used widely without reference to its religious origins.

Wilfrid *(Wilfred)*

An Old English name arising from the compound of *'will'* (will) and *'frith'* (peace) so 'strong peacemaker'. There were two eighth-century Anglo-Saxon saints of this name; the better known (whose name may have been Waldfridus) played a leading role at the groundbreaking Synod of Whitby (664) and spread the gospel among the Frisians and South Saxons. Not so often used nowadays, the name was very popular in the nineteenth century and early part of the twentieth century.

12 October

Will

Short form of 'William' *(see William)*.

William

From the Old German 'Willahelm' meaning 'determined protector'. It was introduced into England by the Normans and quickly became one of the commonest male names in the country. A truly European name it is found throughout Europe ('Gulielmus' Latin; 'Guillaume' French; 'Guillermo' Spanish; 'Gulielmo' Italian). There were over forty-five saints, mostly in the medieval period, but none were particularly well-known.

(St William of York) 8 June

X

Xavier
Of uncertain origin, possibly Spanish with Arabic antecedents, meaning 'bright'. It was the surname of the Spanish saint, St Francis Xavier, one of the first members of the Society of Jesus (Jesuits) and an amazingly successful missionary in the Far East. He is reputed to have converted, before modern times, more people to Christianity than anyone else. The name is used almost exclusively in the Roman Catholic community.

3 Decembe

Z

Zacharias *(Zachariah, Zachary)*
From the Hebrew meaning 'Jehovah has remembered'. There was a king of Israel of this name and it is the name of John the Baptist's father (Luke 1:13), the Jewish priest who received a vision in the temple. There is only one noteworthy saint bearing this name; he was the Greek Pope who was forthright in pushing through Church reforms in the eighth century. He died in 752. Zachary became a common form of Zacharias in the sixteenth century, and so he became known as St Zachary. In the East his feast day is on 5 September; in the West it is 15 March.

5 September or 15 March

Girls

A

Abbie

Shortened form of 'Abigail' *(see Abigail)*.

Abigail

From the Hebrew meaning 'father rejoiced'. In the Bible it was the name of the wife of Nabal (1 Samuel 25:3) who became one of King David's wives. David's second sister (2 Samuel 17:25) also bore the name. Popular in seventeenth-century England, it went out of fashion because it became the slang term for a lady's maid; however, it has enjoyed a return to regular use in the twentieth century. Often shortened to 'Abbey' or 'Gail'.

Ada

Originally from the Old German meaning 'prosperous and joyful', it arrived in England in the eighteenth century from Germany and was very popular in the nineteenth century. There was a St Ada, who was the seventh century abbess of Saint-Julien-des-Pres, Mans. It has been used as a shortened form of 'Adelaide' *(see Adelaide)* or 'Adele'.

4 December

Adelaide

Of Germanic origin, meaning 'noble and kind'. The popularity of King William IV's queen led to its general use in Britain in the nineteenth century. There were three saints of this name, the most influential being the widow of the Holy Roman Emperor, Otto the Great (*c*.930–999) who became regent and was revered for her sanctity. Often shortened to 'Addy' or 'Ada' *(see Ada)*.

16 December

Adeline

Introduced into England by the Normans, it originates from the Old German meaning 'noble woman'. In common use in the Middle Ages, there are two little-known saints of that period, one being a French abbess, who was the granddaughter of William the Conqueror.

20 October

Agatha

From the Latin form of the Greek name 'Agathe' meaning 'good'. This was the name of a very famous and popular virgin-martyr, from Palermo, Sicily, of the third century, honoured in both the Eastern and Western Church; hence, a form of the name is found in every European country. Often abbreviated to 'Aggy'.

5 February

Agnes

The Latin version of the Greek name 'Hagne' meaning 'pure'. St Agnes, a fourth-century virgin-martyr, was very popular throughout Christian Europe in the Middle Ages so the name is found in every country ('Agnes' French; 'Agnese' Italian; 'Inez' Spanish). There are four later saints of the same name. From the twelfth to the sixteenth century, it was one of the most common girls name used in England.

21 January

Aileen *(See Eileen)*.

Aimee *(Amy)*

From the French word *'aimer'* meaning 'to love'. So originally it was a nickname meaning 'beloved'. There is, however, a male saint with this name; a seventh-century French abbot.

13 September

Alberta

The female form of 'Albert' *(see Albert)*.

Albina *(Albinia)*

Derived from the Latin word *'albus'* meaning 'white'. Common in Italy, the name was first used in England in the sixteenth century. Not often used in the twenty-first century, it originates from a St Albina, a young virgin-martyr of the third century.

16 December

Alex *(Alexa)*

A female form of 'Alexander' *(see Alexander)*.

Alexandra *(Alexandria)*

A female form of 'Alexander' *(see Alexander)*.

Alexia

The female form of 'Alexis' *(see Alexis)*.

Alice

From the Old French and a variant of 'Adelaide'. In the twelfth century in France and England it was appearing as 'Alicia' or 'Alesia'. It dropped out of use in seventeenth century England, but was revived by Romance writers in the nineteenth century *(see Adelaide)*.

Alicia *(Alesia)* *(See Alice).*

Alison
In thirteenth-century France it was a familiar form of 'Alice' *(see Alice).*

Anastasia
From the Russian, and a popular name in Eastern Europe. It is derived from the Greek male name 'Anastasios' which comes from the Greek for 'resurrection'. There are twenty-seven male saints of the name 'Anastasius', including two popes. Of the four female saints, the most famous is the fourth-century martyr who died at Sirmium in Dalmatia.
25 December

Andrea
The female form of 'Andrew' *(see Andrew).*

Angel
Until recently this has been an exclusively male name (e.g. 'Angelo' is a common male name in Italy). It comes from the Greek word *'angelos'* which in the New Testament means 'messenger from God'. There are several little-known male saints of this name (no female saints). Through its use as a female name in the Afro- American community, it has entered Britain as a female name.
5 May

Angela
The original female form of the male name 'Angel' or 'Angelus' *(see Angel).* There was a famous St Angela de Merici (1474–1540) who devoted her life to the education

of girls (at a time when it was considered a waste of time to do so). This led to the foundation of the first Roman Catholic teaching order (1535), the Ursulines, specially dedicated to the education of girls.

27 January

Angelica
Derived from the Latin, feminine form of 'Angelus' *(see Angel and Angela)*.

Angelina
A variant form of 'Angela' or 'Angelica' *(see Angela)*.

Angie
Familiar form of 'Angela' *(see 'Angela')*.

Anita
From the Spanish form 'Ana' or 'Ann' *(see Ann)*.

Ann *(Anna, Anne)*
From the Hebrew name 'Hanna' *(see Hannah)*. This was the name, according to tradition, (not recorded in the Bible or any reliable source) of the mother of the Virgin Mary. It was the great popularity of this 'saint' in the Middle Ages throughout the whole of Europe, that made it such a popular name in all European countries.

26 July

Annette
In France the familiar form of 'Ann'. In the English-

speaking world it has become a name, in the twentieth century, in its own right *(see Ann)*.

Annie
Familiar form of 'Ann' *(see Ann)*.

Antoinette
This is the French, feminine form of 'Antoine', in English 'Antony' *(see Antony)*.

Antonia
This is the Italian, feminine form of Antony *(see Antony)*. There were two fifteenth-century saintly Italian women of this name: Antonia of Florence (a) and Antonia of Brescia (b).

(a) 28 February, (b) 27 October

Ariadne
From the Greek meaning 'holy one'. In Greek mythology she was the daughter of the Cretan king, Minos, who helped Theseus to escape the labyrinth. The name survived into Christian times because of St Ariadne, who died in Phrygia for her faith in 130 AD.

17 September

Audrey
From the Anglo-Saxon, derived from the Old English name 'Etheldreda' meaning 'strong and noble' *(see Etheldreda)*.

Audrina
A variant of 'Audrey' *(see Audrey)*.

Augusta

The feminine form of 'Augustus' or 'Augustine'. From the Latin meaning 'sacred and majestic' *(see Augustine)*. In the fifth century there was a virgin-martyr of this name.

27 March

Aurelia

From the Latin word *'aureus'* meaning 'golden'. It was a Roman family name and also the name of three little-known saints of the early years of Christianity. Unknown in medieval England, although used in France. Interest in the name was revived in the seventeenth century.

15 October

Ava

Probably from the Old German; the meaning is uncertain. There was a ninth-century saint of this name who was the daughter of the great King Pepin; she became abbess of Denain in Hainault. Modern interest in the name stems from the film star, Ava Gardner.

29 April

Averil *(Avril)*

From the Old English meaning 'slayer of the boar'. Used throughout the Middle Ages, it was the name of a little-known, fifth-century Yorkshire saint.

24 May

B

Barbara

A popular European name (e.g. 'Barbe' French; 'Varvara' Russian). From the Greek for 'strange' or 'foreign'. St Barbara, a third-century Syrian virgin-martyr, was highly regarded in the Middle Ages but modern research casts doubts upon her historical existence. Legend has it, that for her faith, she was shut up in a tower and later killed by her father. He was, in turn, struck by lightning. As a result Barbara became patron saint of firework makers and protectress against lightning and fire.

4 December

Bea

Short form of 'Beatrice' or 'Beatrix' *(see Beatrix)*.

Beatrice

This is the French and Italian form of 'Beatrix' *(see Beatrix)*.

Beatrix

From the Latin meaning 'bringer of joy'. It was a popular name throughout Europe during the Middle Ages (e.g. 'Beatrice' French and Italian; 'Beatriz' Spanish). There were several saintly women of this name, particularly the fourth-century Roman martyr and the fifteenth-century abbess of Toledo. The name went out of fashion in the seventeenth century, but was revived again in the nineteenth (e.g. Beatrix Potter).

16 August

Becca
Short form of 'Rebecca' *(see Rebecca)*.

Becky
Familiar form of 'Rebecca' *(see Rebecca)*.

Bella
Short form of 'Isabella' *(see Isabella)*.

Benedicta
From the Latin *'benedictus'* meaning 'blessed'. It is the feminine version of 'Benedict' *(see Benedict)*. This male name was very common throughout medieval Christian Europe; consequently there are five rather obscure female saints with the name 'Benedicta'.

17 August

Bernadette
This is the French feminine diminutive form of 'Bernard' *(see Bernard)*. Mostly used by members of the Catholic community in honour of St Bernadette of Lourdes (1844–1879), the poor young French girl who had a series of visions of the Virgin Mary in her home town of Lourdes.

16 April

Bernice
This is the modern version of 'Berenice'. It comes from the Greek and means 'bringer of victory'. The name is found in the Bible in Acts 25:13; she is the sister of King Agrippa and later mistress of the Emperor Titus. It was also borne by a little-known fourth-century Syrian martyr. The name was first used in England by the Puritans of the seventeenth century, and taken by them to the USA where it is still in common use.

4 October

Bertha

From the Latin version of the Frankish name, meaning 'bright and shining'. Not in fashion now, it was in regular use during the Middle Ages. Three saints bore the name, the most interesting being the sixth-century daughter of the king of the Franks who became the first Christian queen of England. As queen of Kent she welcomed the missionary from Rome, St Augustine, who became the first Archbishop of Canterbury.

24 March

Bess

Short form of 'Elizabeth' *(see Elizabeth)*.

Beth

Short form of 'Elizabeth' *(see Elizabeth)*.

Bethany

One of the very few modern Christian names to come into vogue in recent times. It is taken from the place in the New Testament (John 11:1; 12:1), a village just outside Jerusalem, where Lazarus, Martha and Mary lived; and where Jesus stayed during the last week of his life (Holy Week). It is from the Hebrew and probably means 'house of figs'.

Betty

Short form of 'Elizabeth' *(see Elizabeth)*.

Beulah

From the Hebrew meaning 'the married one'. It is a biblical name applied by the prophet Isaiah to the land of Israel (Isaiah 62:4). It was taken up by the Puritans of the seventeenth century, as they looked for new names to avoid using the traditional saints' names, which they rejected as 'Catholic'.

Bianca

From the Italian *'bianca'* meaning 'white'; it is a variant form of 'Blanche' *(see Blanche)*.

Biddy

The short form, used mainly in Ireland, for 'Bridget' *(see Bridget)*.

Blanche

From the French, being the feminine of the adjective *'blanc'* meaning 'white'. Introduced into England by the Normans, the name was more commonly used in its Latin form 'Candida' *(see Candida)*. There were eight saints of this name; that of most interest was the Devon saint (no firm dates) whose original shrine, surviving the destruction of the Reformation period, is found in the church and village named after her, Whit(e)church, Devon.

1 June

Brenda

This name originates from the Shetland Islands and it is probably the feminine form of the Norse name 'Brand' meaning 'fiery'. However, in Ireland where it has been popular, it's used as the female version of 'Brendan'. He was one of the three most renowned saints in Ireland *(see Brendan)*.

16 May

Bride

A short form of 'Bridget' *(see Bridget)*.

Bridget

The English form, via the French 'Brigette', of the Irish 'Brighid'; later 'Bright' or 'Brigid'. Originally it was the name of an ancient Celtic goddess (meaning 'the high or exalted one') but it became a very common name in Ireland and England because of the popularity of St Bridget (*c.*450–525) the second patron – after St Patrick – of Ireland. There is also a fourteenth-century St Bridget of Sweden. She founded the first Religious house for women in Ireland. Her popularity in medieval England is attested by the part of the City of London, Bridewell, being named after her.

1 February

Brigitte *(Brigette)*

The French form of 'Bridget' *(see Bridget)*.

Britt

The Swedish form of 'Bridget' *(see Bridget)*.

C

Caitlin *(Caitrin)*
The Gaelic form of 'Catherine' *(see Catherine)*.

Candace *(Candice)*
From the Latin *'canditia'* meaning 'whiteness' or 'pure'. Originally it was a dynastic title of the queens of Ethiopia. The name is found in the New Testament, referring to an Ethiopian queen in Acts 8:27 when the deacon, Philip, baptises her eunuch.

Candida
From the Latin meaning 'white'. The name also appears in its French form 'Blanche' *(see Blanche)*. One of the eight saints who bore this name was, according to legend, an aged woman who in 78 AD welcomed the apostle Peter to Naples on his way to Rome and was healed by him.

4 September

Carla
Feminine form of 'Carl' *(see Carl)*.

Carlotta
The Italian form of 'Charlotte' *(see Charlotte)*.

Carmel *(Carmela)*
From the Hebrew meaning 'garden'. It is the name of a mountain near Haifa in northern Israel, inhabited from early Christian times by hermits. These hermits were

eventually organised into a religious association that became the Carmelite Order. 'Our Lady of Mount Carmel' is an ancient title accorded to the Virgin Mary; there is an old church dedicated to her on the mountain. The name is principally found in the Roman Catholic community.

Carmen

The Spanish form of 'Carmel' *(see Carmel)*.

Carol

The English version of 'Carolus', Latin for 'Charles'. It probably started as a short form of 'Caroline' *(see Caroline)*, also derived 'Carolus' *(see Charles)*.

Carole

The French form of 'Carol' *(see Carol)*.

Caroline *(Carolyn)*

From the Italian feminine form of 'Charles'. Introduced into Britain by King George II's queen, Caroline of Brandenburg; hence, it was a popular name in the eighteenth century *(see Charles)*.

Cath

Shortened form of 'Catherine' *(see Catherine)*.

Catherine *(Catharine)*

Variant form of the original name 'Katherine' *(see Katherine)* from the Latin 'Katerina' and later 'Katharina'. Derived from the Greek word *'katharos'* meaning 'pure'. There are eight saints of this name witnessing to its popularity in the Middle Ages. Little is known about the original St Katherine (d.*c*.310), a virgin-martyr of Alexandria, except the legend that she was tortured on a spiked wheel (a) (the origin of the firework called a Catherine wheel). A more important figure was St Catherine of Siena (1347–1380) a mystic and reformer who exerted a powerful influence upon the political and religious scene of her time (b).

(a) 25 November, (b) 29 April

Cathleen

A variant spelling of 'Kathleen' *(see Kathleen)*.

Cathy

Familiar form of 'Catherine' *(see Catherine)*.

Catrin

The Welsh form of 'Catherine' *(see Catherine)*.

Cecilia

A popular European name (e.g. 'Cecile' French; 'Cacile' German) throughout history, it originates from the Latin 'Caecilia', the feminine of 'Caecilius' *(see Cecil)*. The name acquired its fame from the second to the third century Roman virgin-martyr, who is for no accountable reason, the patroness of music. The name was introduced into England by the Normans; William the Conqueror named his daughter after the saint.

22 November

Celeste

From the Latin *'caelestis'* meaning 'heavenly'; the name was more common in France than elsewhere. It was used by the early Christians but there is no well-known saint of this name.

Chantal *(Chantel, Chantelle)*

Originally a French place name, its popularity and use as a given name, comes from St Jane Francis de Chantal (1572–1641) who lived at Chantal, close to Saône-et-Loire. As a widow, under the guidance of St Francis de Sales, she founded the Religious Order of the Visitation and had sixty-six convents under her guidance at her death.

12 December

Charis

From the Greek word *'kharis'* meaning 'grace'. The idea of God's grace (his love and generosity) being available to everyone was the central teaching of the New Testament, but as a name it was not in use until after the Reformation. It first appeared in the seventeenth century. The use of the name has been reinforced in the latter part of the twentieth century due to renewed Christian interest in the charisms bestowed by God and promoted by the Charismatic Renewal Movement.

Charissa

A variant of 'Charis' *(see Charis)*.

Charity

The name comes from the French *'charite'*, but originally from the Latin *'caritas'*, meaning 'love' or 'charity'. Its use as a given name was inspired by St Paul's description of love in his letter to the Christians of Corinth (1 Corinthians 13). It appeared after the Reformation and was popular in Victorian times.

Charlene *(Charline)*
A modern name found mostly in Australia and the USA; derived from the male 'Charles' with the feminine suffix *(see Charles)*.

Charlotte
Originally from the Italian 'Carlotta', being the feminine version of 'Carlo' (Charles). Not used in Britain before the seventeenth century, it became particularly popular on account of Queen Charlotte (1744–1818), the wife of George III *(see Charles)*.

Cherry
Familiar form of 'Charity' *(see Charity)*.

Chiara
The Italian form of 'Clare' or 'Clara' *(see Clara and Clare)*.

Chloe
From the Greek *'knloe'* meaning 'fresh young blossom'. Not used until the time of the seventeenth-century Puritans, who having destroyed any figures or pictures of the saints found in English parish churches, refused to use their names for their children. Instead they searched the Bible for fresh names. They found a passing reference to a certain 'Chloe' in 1 Corinthians 1:11 and a new Christian name came into use. It has remained more popular than most names introduced at that time.

Chris
Short form of 'Christine' and associated names *(see Christine)*.

Christa
The Latin short form of 'Christine' *(see Christine)*.

Christabel
Although it is found in the seventeenth century, derived from 'Christine', with the suffix '-bel', its popularity appears to spring from Coleridge's poem 'Christabel' (1816) *(see Christine)*.

Christiana *(Christianna)*
The feminine form of 'Christian' *(see Christian and Christine)*.

Christina
From the Latin feminine form of 'Christianus' *(see Christian)*. There are five saints of this name; none of them well-known. All were virgins; two died for their Christian faith and the remainder were saintly nuns.

24 July

Christine *(Christene)*
From the French form of 'Christina', which in turn is from the Latin 'Christianus' meaning 'Christian'. It was rarely used in England before the end of the nineteenth century *(see Christian)*.

Cicely
A variant form of 'Cecily' which is derived from 'Cecilia' *(see Cecilia)*.

Claire

The French form of 'Clara' or 'Clare'. The Normans introduced it into England, but it went out of use; to be revived again in the nineteenth century, when it became very popular *(see Clare)*.

Clara

From the feminine of the Latin word *'clarus'* meaning 'bright' or 'clear'. Its use in thirteenth-century England sprang from the existence of six saints of the name 'Clarus', all early and all associated with France (e.g. St Clair, a town in Normandy). The English version of 'Clare' became more common.

4 November

Clare

The English form of 'Clara' (the Italian 'Chiara'). In later Christian times it became very popular because of the devotion and honour given to St Clare of Assisi (*c.*1194–1253), the influential friend of St Francis of Assisi. Inspired by St Francis, she was as devoted to the poor as he was and founded the Poor Clares Order. She governed the Order for forty years and was consulted by popes, cardinals and bishops.

11 August

Clarice *(Clarisse, Clarissa)*

A French derivative of 'Clara' which was almost certainly brought to England by the Normans; its first recorded use being in 1199. It continued to be popular throughout the twelfth and thirteenth centuries, but rarely found since *(see Clara and Clare)*.

Claudia

From the feminine of the Latin name 'Claudius' *(see Claude)* meaning 'lame'. The name appears among a group of converts of St Paul in 2 Timothy 4:21. It was used by the Puritans in the seventeenth century in their campaign to rid the country of traditional names, replacing them with new biblical names for their children. There were two early Christian martyrs of this name.

7 August

Claudine

From the French feminine diminutive form of 'Claude' *(see Claude)*.

Clemence *(Clemency)*

From the Latin *'clementia'* meaning 'mildness'. It appears to have been used as the feminine form of the male name 'Clement' *(see Clement)*.

Clementina *(Clementine)*

Further feminine forms of 'Clement'. First used in the nineteenth century and grew in popularity, but rarely used in modern times *(see Clement)*.

Colette

Originates from the French name 'Nicolette' which is the diminutive of 'Nicole', the French feminine form of 'Nicholas' *(see Nicholas)*. There is a St Colette (originally Nicolette Boilet, 1381–1447) famous for reforming the Poor Clares Order and helping St Vincent Ferrer to resolve the Papal Schism.

6 March

Columbine

From the Italian 'Colombina', which comes from *'columba'* meaning 'dove'. It can be regarded as the feminine version of the male name 'Columba', from the famous Scottish missionary saint of the sixth centuy *(see Columba)*. However, the modern use of the name springs from a nineteenth-century practice, inspired by the Romantic movement in literature, of coining new female names from flowers and nature. The columbine is a flower of the aquilegia family with five spurred petals.

9 June

Connie

Familiar form of 'Constance' *(see Constance)*.

Constance

The English form of the Latin word *'constantia'* meaning 'constancy'. Also the feminine of the male name 'Constantius' or 'Constantine'. Introduced into England by the Normans, it was common throughout the Middle Ages. There were several saints with the name 'Constantine', the most important being the emperor who died in 337 and one first-century martyr named 'Constantia' who died with a St Felix, at Nocera, Italy.

19 September

Consuelo

From the Spanish for 'counsel', taken from the title of the Blessed Virgin Mary, 'Our Lady of Good Counsel'. Used in Spanish-speaking parts of Central and South America and occasionally in the Roman Catholic community in Britain.

19 September

Cornelia

The Latin, feminine form of 'Cornelius' *(see Cornelius)*. There are two saintly women of this name; a martyr who in the third century died for her faith with Theodulus in North Africa. In the nineteenth century the American nun, Cornelia Connelly, founded the public school for girls at Mayfield, East Sussex.

31 March

Cristina

The form of 'Christina' found in Spain, Italy and Portugal *(see Christina)*.

Damaris
A Greek name found in the Bible (Acts 17:34): an Athenian woman convert of St Paul. Its meaning is not certain. This was one of the names that the Puritans of the seventeenth century discovered in the Bible and introduced into England. Very occasionally found, particularly in the USA, in modern times.

Daniela
From the Latin feminine form of 'Daniel' *(see Daniel)*.

Danielle
From the French feminine form of 'Daniel' *(see Daniel)*.

Daria
The feminine form of the male 'Darius' (not now in use). There was a St Daria who died at Rome for her Christian faith in 283 with her Egyptian husband, Chrysanthus; they were buried in a catacomb on the Via Salaria.

25 October

Davina *(Davinia)*
The feminine form of 'David' originating from Scotland *(see David)*. It could also be the feminine form of 'Davinus'; the saint of this name was an Armenian who died in 1051 at Lucca, Italy.

3 June

Deborah

From the Hebrew for 'bee'. It was the name of one of the great female figures of the Old Testament of the Bible. She was a judge and prophetess (Judges 4–5). It was also the name of Rebecca's nurse (Genesis 35:8). Always a popular Jewish name, it was adopted by the seventeenth-century Puritans. It has retained its popularity and is often shortened to 'Debbie' or 'Debra', which have become names in their own right.

Delilah

A biblical name but its origins are uncertain. It is given the meaning 'gentle temptress' from the actions of the Delilah who tempted Samson (Judges 16:4–20). It was the seventeenth-century Puritans who introduced the name into Britain and the USA; but it is rarely used in the twenty-first century.

Delores

A variant form of 'Dolores' *(see Dolores)*.

Delphine

French name taken from the Latin 'Delphina' meaning 'woman from Delphi'. There was a rather obscure St Delphinus, a fifth-century bishop of Bordeaux; also a fourteenth-century saintly noblewoman, Delphina, from Languedoc.

9 December

Denise

Originally from the Latin 'Dionysia', this is the French feminine form of 'Dennis' *(see Dennis)*.

Desiree

French name taken from the Latin *'desiderata'* meaning 'desired'. In early Christian times it was given to a child who had been longed for. There are four male saints of the name 'Desideratus', none of them well known.

8 May

Diana

From the Latin name of the moon goddess, the equivalent of the Greek goddess, Artemis. The name appears in the Bible (Acts 19:24–41) when St Paul becomes involved in riots stirred up by worshippers of Diana of the Ephesians. It was not generally considered suitable as a Christian name, and does not appear in common use until after the sixteenth century. However, there was a twelfth-century saintly Dominican nun of Bologna, of this name. The French form 'Diane' has become more established since the middle of the twentieth century.

10 June

Diane

The French form of 'Diana' *(see Diana)*.

Dinah *(Dina)*

From the Hebrew meaning 'judgement'. In the Bible she is the daughter of Jacob by Leah (Genesis 34). Not used until the seventeenth century, it was then popular until the nineteenth century when it was replaced by 'Diane' or 'Diana'.

Dolores

A Spanish name taken from the title of the Virgin Mary, 'Maria de los Dolores' meaning 'Mary of the Sorrows'. An ancient devotion to the Seven Sorrows of the Virgin Mary was formalised by the Roman Catholic Church when it instituted (1423) a feast day for 'Our Lady of Sorrows' annually on 15 September. Widely used in the English-speaking world, particularly among American Roman Catholics.

15 September

Dominica

From the Latin, the feminine form of 'Dominic' *(see Dominic)*.

Dominque

The French feminine form of 'Dominic' *(see Dominic)*.

Donna

A modern name, originating from the USA, not in use until the 1920s. It comes from 'Madonna' a title accorded to the Blessed Virgin Mary, particularly in Spanish and Italian communities *(see Madonna)*.

Dorcas

From the Greek *'dorkas'* meaning 'gazelle' or 'graceful'. It was used by the Christians of the first few centuries because of the good widow of Joppa (also known as 'Tabitha') who was raised to life by Peter (Acts 9:32–43). It dropped out of use in the Middle Ages but was enthusiastically revived by the seventeenth-century Puritans who took it to the USA *(see Tabitha)*.

25 October

Doris

From the Greek meaning 'from the sea'. It appears in Greek mythology as the name of a minor goddess of the sea. There were several, very obscure, early Christian martyrs of this name; however, the name only really came into use in the nineteenth century.

Dorothea

The feminine form of the male Latin name 'Dorotheus' meaning 'gift of God'. There were five male saints of this name, all before the eleventh century, and three female saints; the best known being the virgin-martyr who died (c.300) at Caesarea, Palestine, in the reign of the Emperor Diocletian.

6 February

Dorothy

The English form of 'Dorothea' *(see Dorothea)*.

Drusilla

From the Latin meaning 'the strong one'. It was the name of one of St Paul's converts, the wife of the Roman Governor, Felix (Acts 24:24). The Puritans of the seventeenth century, in their drive to find new biblical names for their children, were the first to use it in Western Christianity.

Dymphna

This is the English version of the Irish 'Damhnait', which is of uncertain meaning. Very little is known of the Irish virgin-saint of this name. As many cases of epilepsy and insanity were believed to have been cured at her shrine in Belgium, she became patroness of the mentally ill.

15 May

E

Edith

From the Old English 'Eadgyth' coming from the two words *'ead'* (riches) and *'gyth'* (war). It was a popular Saxon name, which survived the Norman Conquest, with two saints, Edith of Polesworth (d.925) and Edith of Wilton (961–984), the daughter of King Edgar. In the twentieth century, there was St Edith Stein (1891–1942) the Polish Carmelite nun and theologian who died heroically in the gas chambers of Auschwitz.

(St Edith Stein) 9 August

Edna

From the Hebrew meaning 'pleasure', it is found in the apocryphal books of the Bible as the wife of Enoch; also in the Book of Tobit, as the mother of Sarah (7:14). It appears to have come into England in the eighteenth century from Ireland where it is more commonly found.

Edwina

The modern female form of 'Edwin' *(see Edwin)*.

Eileen *(Aileen)*

An Irish name that became popular in Britain at the beginning of the twentieth century. It is thought to be the Irish equivalent of 'Helen' *(see Helen)*, but may equally have evolved from 'Evelyn'.

Elaine

An Old French form of 'Helen' *(see Helen)*. As an independent name, it is found in the fifteenth-century legend of King Arthur (*Morte D'Arthur*) by Thomas Malory but there is no evidence of common use before the nineteenth century.

Eleanor

From the Old French name 'Alienor' and always thought to be a form of 'Helen' *(see Helen)*, but this is now questioned by scholars. Certainly introduced into England by Eleanor of Aquitaine (1122–1204) wife of King Henry II. The name is found with various spellings, e.g. 'Elinor'; 'Elianor'.

Elena

The Spanish and Italian form of 'Helen' *(see Helen)*.

Eleonora

The Italian form of 'Eleanor' *(see Eleanor)*.

Elfreda *(Elfleda)*

This is the later form of the two Old English names, with no clear modern meaning. There were three saints, all before the Norman Conquest, and all Benedictine nuns. It was also the name of one of King Alfred the Great's daughters. The name went out of fashion but enjoyed a revival of interest in the nineteenth century.

8 February

Elise

The French short form of 'Elizabeth' *(see Elizabeth)*.

Eliza

Short form of 'Elizabeth' first used in the sixteenth century *(see Elizabeth)*.

Elizabeth *(Elisabeth)*

From the Hebrew 'Elisheba' meaning 'consecrated to God'. It was the name of Aaron's wife (Exodus 6:23) and more famously the mother of John the Baptist (Luke 1:60) and cousin of Mary of Nazareth (a). A popular name throughout the whole of Europe, it is usually spelt with a 'z' in Britain, but with an 's' throughout the Continent. There have been five saints bearing the name; the most influential being St Elizabeth of Hungary (b) (1207–1231). St Elizabeth Seton (1774–1821) was renowned in the USA for her work for Catholic education, and for being the first American to be declared a saint (c).

(a) 5 November,
(b) 17 November, (c) 4 January

Ellen

This was originally a variant of 'Helen', but became a name in its own right *(see Helen)*.

Elsa

Shortened form of 'Elizabeth' *(see Elizabeth)*.

Elspeth *(Elsie)*

The Scottish shortened version of 'Elizabeth' *(see Elizabeth)*.

Emily

From the Latin name 'Aemilius', it evolved into its present form due to Teutonic influnces; meaning 'industrious'. There are three French saints of this name, all nuns; not well known outside of France.

17 June

Emma

From the Old German meaning 'one who heals'. It was popular among the Normans and became common in England partly because it was the name of the mother of the king, St Edward the Confessor. It was well used throughout the Middle Ages, often spelt as 'Emm'. There are several little-known saints of this name, sometimes identified as 'Gemma'.

29 June

Erica

The feminine form of 'Eric' *(see Eric).*

Esther

In the book of the Bible of this name, 'Esther' is said to be a Persian name, the equivalent to the Hebrew 'Hadassah' (Esther 2:7). The meaning is not clear, although 'myrtle' and 'star' have both been suggested. Heroine of the Jewish people, Esther saved the Jews from a 'holocaust' planned by the Persian counsellor, Haman. The name is not found in England before the seventeenth century. Its use has spread beyond the Jewish community in modern times.

Ethel

From the Old English, which originated from the Teutonic, meaning 'noble', it is the shortened form of the old traditional Saxon names 'Ethelburga (a); 'Etheldreda' (b); 'Ethelfleda' (c); these were all Anglo-Saxon saints, all noblewomen who founded convents in East Anglia and the south-east of England. The name was revived, in this short form, in the nineteenth century but not often found in recent times.

(a) 5 April, (b) 23 June, (c) 23 October

Etta

Short form of 'Henrietta' or 'Rosetta' *(see Henrietta and Rosetta)*.

Eugenia

The feminine form of 'Eugene' *(see Eugene)*.

Eunice

From the Greek *'eunike'*, a compound of two Greek words, meaning 'good victory' or 'victorious'. It was the name of the mother of Timothy, St Paul's disciple (2 Timothy 1:5). Not found in medieval times, it was introduced by the Puritans of the seventeenth century who were keen to avoid using saints' names for their children.

Eva

The Latin form of 'Eve' *(see Eve)*.

Evangeline

A modern name, apparently invented by the American poet Longfellow (1848) derived from the Greek word *'euangeilon'* or the Latin *'evangelium'* meaning 'good news' or 'gospel'. Hence, the four gospel writers are called 'evangelists'. Common in the USA and occasionally found in Britain.

Eve

The English form of the Latin 'Eva', which comes from the Hebrew 'Havva' (meaning 'living') being the name of the first woman created by God from the rib of Adam (Genesis 2:22). It has been used in England since the thirteenth century.

F

Faith
First used after the Reformation for both girls and boys. It obviously refers to the virtue or quality of believing and trusting in God which is central to Christianity. It was a very popular name among the seventeenth-century Puritans.

Felicia
The Latin female form of 'Felix' *(see Felix)*.

Felicity
The English form of the Latin name 'Felicitas', meaning 'happiness'. A popular feminine name among the Christians of the first few centuries; there are at least five martyrs of this name who died for their faith during the Roman persecutions, especially under the Emperor Diocletian.
23 November

Flora
From the Latin *'flos'* for 'flower' and the Roman goddess of flowers. It appears to have come into England from Scotland in the eighteenth century, through the reputation of Flora MacDonald who helped Bonnie Prince Charles to escape in 1746. Three virgin-martyrs of early Christianity bore the name.
24 November

Florence

From the Latin masculine name 'Florentius' which is derived from *'florens'* meaning 'blooming' or 'flourishing'. It was a popular male name (there are eighteen saintly bishops, abbots and martyrs) but gradually it became exclusively a feminine name, perhaps due to the admiration for Florence Nightingale (1820–1910) who was named after her birth place, the Italian city of Florence.

20 June

Frances

The feminine form of Francis. Originally used for both men and women it did not become distinctively feminine until the seventeenth century. There are two famous saints of this name; St Frances of Rome (a) (1384–1440) and St Frances Xavier Cabrini (1850–1917) foundress of a missionary congregation (b) *(see Francis)*.

(a) 9 March, (b) 22 December

Francesca

The Italian form of 'Frances' *(see Frances)*.

Francine

From the French familiar form of 'Frances' *(see Frances)*.

Freda

Short form of various names ending in '-freda' e.g 'Elfreda' *(see Elfreda)*.

Frederica

The Latin feminine form of 'Frederick' *(see Frederick)*.

G

Gabriela
The Latin feminine form of 'Gabriel' *(see Gabriel)*.

Gabrielle
The French feminine form of 'Gabriel' *(see Gabriel)*.

Gemma
From the Italian *'gemma'* meaning 'a gem'. From the Italian community, the name spread into the wider Roman Catholic use, principally because of St Gemma Galgani (1878–1903) who during her short, but very hard life, had many religious experiences including the stigmata. In recent times the name is more widely found.

11 April

Genette
Variant spelling of 'Jeanette' *(see Jeanette)*.

Genevieve
A French name derived from 'Genovefa'; its meaning is uncertain. St Genevive (422–500) is the patron of Paris. When the city was occupied by the Franks and threatened by Attila and his Huns, Genevieve roused the people to defend their city and defeat the invaders. The name was first used in Britain in the nineteenth century.

3 January

Georgette

The French feminine name taken from 'Georges', the French for 'George' *(see George)*.

Georgia

From the Latin form of 'George'. There was a St Georgia, (d.*c*.500) a French virgin-recluse who lived near Clermont in Auvergne.

15 February

Georgiana

From the Latin form of 'George' *(see George)*.

Georgina

The feminine form of 'George' which became popular in eighteenth-century England when the male name was common *(see George)*.

Geraldine

The feminine form of 'Gerald'. It appears to have been invented by the poet Henry Howard, Earl of Surrey, about 1540 in praise of Lady Elizabeth Fitzgerald *(see Gerald)*.

Germaine

The feminine form of the French name 'Germain' which originates from the Latin *'germanus'* meaning 'brother'. There are fifteen male saints of this name; the one female St Germaine Cousins (1579–1601) was the daughter of a poor farmer who heroically lived a very harsh life near Toulouse, France.

15 June

Gertrude

From the Old German 'Geredrudis' meaning 'spear maiden'. It was the name of one the Valkyries in the Nordic myths; it was borne by three saints, the most important being St Gertrude the Great (c.1256–1302), who had many religious experiences and whose writings on Christian mysticism were very influential. Popular in the nineteenth century, it is rarely found in recent times.

16 November

Gillian

The popular English form of 'Julian(na)'. Commonly found in the Middle Ages; the two spellings became separate names in the seventeenth century *(see Julian)*.

Gina

The short form of 'Georgina' *(see Georgina)*.

Giselle

The French form of 'Gisela' which originates from the German word *'gisl'* meaning 'pledge'. St Gisela (d.1095) was the first queen of Hungary, wife of St Stephen and sister of St Henry, emperor of the Holy Roman Empire.

7 May

Grace

From the Latin *'gracia'* meaning 'grace'. Like 'Faith', 'Hope' and 'Charity', it was introduced after the Reformation by the seventeenth-century Puritans, who were trying to avoid using saints' names for their children. They were probably unaware that there were two little-known saints who bore the name.

5 July

Gwen

The short form of the Welsh name 'Gwendolen' *(see Gwendolen)*.

Gwendolen

A Welsh name meaning 'white-browed girl'. There are various spellings of this ancient Celtic name. There are two fifth-century saints and three a little later in history; all rather obscure. The name appears to have come into use in England in the nineteenth century.

18 October

Hannah

From the Hebrew *'hanna'* meaning 'full of grace'. It was the name of the mother of the prophet Samuel (1 Samuel 1:2). The Greek form of the name 'Anna' *(see Ann)* became well established and widely used throughout Europe. It was the Puritans of the seventeenth century who revived the use of the original form of the name.

Harriet

The English version of the French name 'Henriette' which is the feminine form of 'Henry' *(see Henry)*. It first appeared in seventeenth-century France and became popular in England the following century.

Helen

The English form of the Greek 'Helene', probably derived from the Greek word *'helios'* meaning 'sun' or 'light'. The name of the famous beauty of classical legend, Helen of Troy, but widely used throughout Christian Europe in many varied forms because of St Helena, mother of the first Christian emperor, Constantine (*c*.250–330). She is credited with building many churches in the Holy Land and with the discovery of the remains of the true cross of Christ. Popular from early times in Celtic countries, the traditional English form was 'Ellen'; the current spelling became more popular after the sixteenth century.

18 August

Helena
The Latin form of 'Helen' *(see Helen)*.

Henrietta
The Latin form of the French name 'Henriette' which is the feminine form of 'Henry' *(see Henry)*.

Hilary *(Hillary)*
Originally, and for many centuries, this was a male name coming from the Latin *'hilaris'* meaning 'cheerful' (we still have the word 'hilarious'). There are thirteen saints (all male) including one pope (d.468) and a famous theologian, St Hilary of Poitiers (315–368). It started to be used as a female name in the early twentieth century.

13 January

Hilda
Originally from Germany, the Old English form was *'hild'*, probably derived from the Anglo-Saxon, meaning 'war' or 'battle'. It was borne by the influential Northumbrian abbotess, St Hilda of Whitby (614–680) who convened the important Synod of Whitby which determined the future and form of Christianity in Britain. She has been hailed as 'one of the greatest Englishwomen of all time'.

17 November

Hope
From faith, hope and charity, the fundamental virtues of Christianity. The name was introduced in England, and then the USA, by the Puritans of the seventeenth century. Originally used for both genders, it is now only used as a girl's name.

Hyacinth

The English form of the Greek name 'Hyakinthos', the name of a flower. Until the nineteenth century it was always a male name; there are five male saints, four of them martyrs of the early years of Christianity; the fifth was St Hyacinth (1185–1257) given the title and accolade of 'Apostle of Poland' for his missionary work there. The Romantic movement in Britain in the nineteenth century resulted in the use of the names of flowers being used as girls' names (e.g. 'Rose', 'Lily') at which point the name became a female name.

17 August

I

Ida
From the Old German meaning 'work'. It was brought to England by the Normans but ceased to be used around the fourteenth century; it was revived in the nineteenth century. There are seven little-known saintly women of this name.

4 September

Imelda
From the Greek meaning 'longed for'. Found in its Latin form in use in Italy and Spain, but rarely used in Britain. There was one saint, Imelda Lambertini of Bologna who died in 1333.

12 May

Irene
From the Greek for 'peace'. A common Byzantine name, it was borne by three martyrs of the fourth century and an empress (d.803). It first appeared in England in the nineteenth century and grew in popularity throughout the twentieth century.

5 April

Isabel *(Isobel)*
Originally the Spanish form of 'Elizabeth'. Interchangeable up to the sixteenth century, it had been, throughout the Middle Ages, one of the most popular feminine names; perhaps because it was the name of three English queens *(see Elizabeth)*.

Isidora *(Isadora)*

The feminine form of 'Isidore' *(see Isidore)*.

Ita

Irish name meaning 'desire for truth'. In popular veneration in Ireland, St Ita (d.c.570) ranks second only to St Bridget; many legends exist but there is little reliable history available.

15 January

J

Jacklyn *(Jaclyn)*
Short form of 'Jacquelyn' *(see Jacquelyn)*.

Jacqueline *(Jacquelyn)*
The French feminine of 'Jacques' (James) *(see James)*. Probably introduced into Britain from Flanders; from the thirteenth to the seventeenth century it is found in a variety of forms, e.g. 'Jacklin'.

Jan
Short form of 'Janet' or 'Janice' *(see Janet and Janice)*.

Jane *(Jayne)*
The usual modern form of 'Joanna' (or 'Joan') and the English feminine form of 'John' *(see Joanna, Joan, John)*. Widely found throughout Europe (e.g. 'Giovanna' Italian; 'Juana' Spanish; 'Jeanne' French). Very common in the nineteenth century, it did not appear in England until the sixteenth century and nowadays it is often used in a combination name, e.g. 'Mary-Jane'. There are six saints, all of them foundresses of Religious Orders e.g. St Jane of Valois (1461–1504) who founded the Congregation of the Annunciation (a), and St Jane-Frances de Chantal (1572–1641), the Visitation Sisters (b).

(a) 4 February, (b) 12 September

Janelle
A modern form of 'Jane' *(see Jane)*.

Janet
A diminutive form of 'Jane' *(see Jane)*.

Janette
A modern variant of 'Jane' *(see Jane)*.

Janice *(Janis)*
A modern variant, originating in the USA, of 'Jane' *(see Jane)*.

Jean
Derived from the Old French 'Jehane' (as are 'Jane' and 'Joan') and a feminine form of 'John' *(see John)*. It was, at first, solely found in Scotland; in the twentieth century it has become more widely used.

Jemima *(Jemina)*
From the Hebrew meaning 'dove'. In the Bible it was the name of Job's eldest daughter (Job 42:14). It does not appear to have been used until the seventeenth century; introduced by the Puritans, who loved biblical names.

Jemma
A variant spelling of 'Gemma' *(see Gemma)*.

Joan
The usual feminine form of 'John', from the Old French 'Jehane' or the Latin 'Iohanna' *(see Joanna and John)*. Used throughout the Middle Ages, in the sixteenth century it was the third most common feminine name

in England. Although there is a 'Joanna' mentioned in the New Testament (Luke 8:3), the famous saint of this name is St Joan of Arc (1412–1431) who led the victorious French army against the English, but was burnt to death at the stake when she was captured.

30 May

Joanna *(Johanna)*

From the Greek spelling of the Hebrew name 'Johanna' and in biblical times it was used for men or for women (Luke 3:27; Luke 24:10). Throughout Europe, during the Middle Ages, 'Johanna' was the common feminine form of 'John', this became 'Joanna' and then 'Joan' *(see Joan and John)*.

Joni

A modern version of 'Joanne'; a familiar form of 'Joan' *(see Joan)*.

Josephine

From the French, it is the feminine form of 'Joseph' *(see Joseph)*.

Joy

From the Old French *'joie'* translating the Latin *'gaudia'*, which figures so much in Christian spirituality and thought (in the medieval European Christian calendar one day was known as 'Gaudete Sunday'). Used by the seventeenth-century Puritans, the name went out of fashion until the nineteenth century when it was rediscovered.

Joyce

This was a popular medieval name used for both boys and girls, and appears in England from Norman times in the Norman form 'Josce' meaning 'lord'. Also in the Old English form of 'Jose'. A highly regarded Breton hermit-saint of the seventh century made the name popular. It ceased to be a male name about the fourteenth century.

13 December

Judith

From the Hebrew meaning 'woman from Judea' or 'Jewess'. It was the name of the Jewish heroine who tricked and slew Holofernes, the Assyrian general. The story is found in the Book of Judith in the Apocrypha of the Bible (found in most modern versions.) There was a little-known ninth-century saint of this name. Not in common use in England before the eighteenth century, it has enjoyed popularity in more recent times.

29 June

Julia

The feminine form of 'Julius'. It is found throughout Europe (e.g. 'Julie' French; 'Giulia' Italian; etc) although it did not appear in common use until the sixteenth century. St Paul in his letter to the Romans (16:15) refers to a follower of this name, and there are seven early Christian martyrs. There is also St Julia Billart (1751–1816) the foundress of the schools and Sisters of Notre Dame.

8 April

Juliana

The feminine form of 'Julianus'. A popular name in early Christian times, there are seven martyrs, and between the thirteenth and the fifteenth centuries it was one of the most common names; there are four saintly women from this period, including the famous Juliana (or Julian) of Norwich (d.1423) one of the most celebrated of English mystics. She was an anchoress who took her name from the church to which her cell was attached *(see Julian)*.

13 May

Julie

The French form of 'Julia' *(see Julia)*.

Juliet

The English form of the French name 'Juliette', which is the diminutive of 'Julia' *(see Julia)*.

Justina *(Justine)*

The feminine form of 'Justin' *(see Justin)*.

Karen *(Karin)*
The Danish form of 'Katherine'. Introduced into the USA, and then to Britain, imported by Scandinavian immigrants *(see Katherine)*.

Katarina
The Swedish form of 'Katherine' *(see Katherine)*.

Katerina
The Russian form of 'Katherine' *(see Katherine)*.

Katherine
The English alternative spelling *(see Catherine)* of the Greek name 'Aikaterine', the meaning of which is thought to be 'pure'.

Kathleen
From 'Caitlin', the Irish version of 'Catherine' *(see Catherine)*.

Katya
The familiar form of the Russian 'Yekaterina' (Katherine) *(see Katherine)*.

Keren
From the Hebrew meaning 'horn of eye-paint'. It is a shortened form of the name borne by Job's youngest daughter, 'Keren-Happuch' (Job 42:14).

Kirsten

The Scandinavian form of 'Christine' *(see Christine)*.

Kristen

The Danish form of 'Christine' *(see Christine)*.

Kristina

The Swedish form of 'Christine' *(see Christine)*.

L

Laura

The feminine form of the Latin name 'Laurus' meaning 'laurel'; or possibly the feminine form of 'Laurence'. There was a St Laura, a ninth-century Spanish nun, killed by the Moors for her Christian faith. The name probably came into Britain from Italy, and was rarely used before the nineteenth century.

19 October

Lauren (*Loren*)

A modern name; a feminine form of 'Laurence' *(see Laurence)*.

Leah

From the Hebrew meaning 'the weary one'. It was the name of the sister of Rachel (Genesis 29:16–35) who was married off to Jacob by Laban. It was used first by the Puritans of the seventeenth century; who also took it to the USA.

Lena

A shortened form of 'Helena' *(see Helen)*.

Leonora

A shortened form of 'Eleonora' *(see Eleonora)*.

Lilian (*Lillian*)

The origin is uncertain but it is generally believed to be derived from 'Elizabeth' *(see Elizabeth)*.

Lois

Probably a Greek name, its origins and meaning are unknown. It was the name of the grandmother of Timothy, the disciple of St Paul (2 Timothy 1:5). It was adopted by the seventeenth-century Puritans when they rejected the use of traditional names derived from the saints.

Lola

Originally a Spanish short form of 'Dolores' *(see Dolores)*.

Lora

The German form of 'Laura' *(see Laura)*.

Loreto

Mainly found in the Roman Catholic community; it is inspired by devotion to the Blessed Virgin Mary, under the title 'Our Lady of Loretto'. The place is a town in Italy where, legend has it, in the thirteenth century, the house of the Holy Family of Nazareth was transported by angels.

Loretta

A variant form of 'Loreto' *(see Loreto)*.

Louisa

The Latin feminine form of 'Louis'. Sometimes used as an alternative spelling for 'Louise' *(see Louis and Louise)*.

Louise

The French feminine form of 'Louis' *(see Louis)*. There is a renowned French saint of this name. St Louise de Marillac (1591–1660), a widow who became a nun and helped St Vincent de Paul to found the Sisters of Charity (1638). Not used in Britain before the seventeenth century; however, by the end of the twentieth century it had become one of the most popular girls' names.

Lucia

The Latin feminine form of 'Lucius' meaning 'light'. There are eighteen little-known saints of early Christian times with the name 'Lucius'; five female saints named 'Lucia' (or 'Lucy') the most famous being the Sicilian virgin-martyr, St Lucy of Syracuse (a) (d.304). The most modern saint is Lucy, a Chinese school teacher beheaded at Kuy-tszheu, in 1862, for her Christian faith (b).

(a) 13 December, (b) 19 February

Lucilla

A Latin familiar form of 'Lucia' *(see Lucia)*. There was a third-century Roman martyr of this name.

25 August

Lucy

The modern form of 'Lucia' from the Old French 'Lucie' *(see Lucia)*.

Ludmilla *(Ludmila)*

From a Slavonic name meaning 'beloved of the people'. It originates from Eastern European countries where its use is inspired by St Ludmilla (d.921) the Duchess of Bohemia, who brought up and educated the young St Wenceslaus. She was brutally murdered because of her Christian faith.

16 September

Lydia

From the Greek meaning 'cultured one' or 'woman from Lydia'. St Lydia, from Thyatira (now Ak-Hissar), was 'a dealer in purple cloth' and St Paul's first European convert (Acts 16:14). The name was first used in the seventeenth century.

3 August

M

Madelaine *(Medeleine, Madeline, Madelyn, Madoline)*
From the Hebrew meaning 'woman from Magdala' (a village formerly on the shores of the Sea of Galilee). The English form comes from the French 'Madeleine' referring to Mary Magdalen (the repentant sinner disciple of Jesus). In all four gospels she is portrayed as one of the most devoted followers of Christ. Several little-known saints were named after her.
22 July

Madonna
A modern name originating from the Italian title of the Blessed Virgin Mary, meaning 'my lady' and used often for example Renaissance paintings and sculptures of the Virgin Mary. It appeared first – and remained popular – among the nineteenth-century Italian immigrants to the USA; made famous by the pop star from such a background, Madonna Ciccone.

Magdalen *(See Madelaine).*

Mair
The Welsh form of 'Mary' *(see Mary).*

Maire
The Irish form of 'Mary' *(see Mary).*

Mairead
The Irish form of 'Margaret' *(see Margaret).*

Maisie

The Scottish familiar form, derived from 'Mairead', or 'Margaret' *(see Margaret)*.

Manuela

From the Spanish feminine form of 'Emmanuel' *(see Emmanuel)* meaning 'God is with us'.

Marcella

The feminine form of the Latin name 'Marcellus', of which there are three saints, including one pope. The name originally meant 'belonging to Mars' (the god, not the planet). There are two saints of this name, the better-known was a saintly widow of Rome (325–410) tortured and executed by the Goths.

31 January

Marcia

The feminine form of 'Mark', from the Latin name 'Marcus'. There were three early Christian martyrs of this name, about whom little is known *(see Mark)*.

Margaret

The English form has come from the French 'Marguerite' which comes from the Latin; however, the name originally appears to be Persian, meaning 'pearl'. It was one of the most widely used female names throughout Europe and continuously popular in England since the Norman Conquest. The first St Margaret, known as 'Marina' in the Eastern Church, was beheaded at Antioch in the third century for her Christian faith. There have been eight further saints including the famous St Margaret of Scotland (a) (*c.*1045–1093), St Margaret

Mary Alacoque (b) (1647–1690) and the butcher's wife of York, St Margaret Clitherow who died for her Catholic faith in 1586 (c).

(a) 16 November,
(b) 16 October, (c) 21 October

Margery

The common medieval form of 'Margaret' *(see Margaret)*.

Marguerite

The French form of 'Margaret' *(see Margaret)*. There is one saint of this name, Marguerite Bourjeoys (1620–1700) the French-born nun who founded the Sisters of Notre Dame de Montreal and their schools, which spread extensively in the USA.

19 January

Maria

The Latin form of 'Mary' *(see Mary)*.

Marianne

An extended spelling of 'Marian'; thought of as a combination of 'Mary' and 'Ann' but not originally so.

Marie

The French form of 'Mary'. Usually pronounced with the emphasis on the end of the word in the French fashion; alternatively with the accent on the first syllable *(see Mary)*.

Mariella

An Italian form of 'Maria' *(see Mary)*.

Marietta

An Italian form of 'Maria' *(see Mary)*.

Marilyn

A modern form, from the USA, of 'Mary' *(see Mary)*.

Marina

The Latin form of the Greek word 'Pelagia', although sometimes believed to be the feminine of 'Marinus' (there are eleven saints of this name) which is the Latin for 'of the sea'. Little is known of the two early Christian saints of this name.

18 July

Marion *(Marian)*

Originally a diminutive of 'Mary'. It was used throughout the Middle Ages and later, probably in the eighteenth-century, led to the spelling 'Marian' *(see Mary)*.

Marisa *(Marissa)*

A modern variant of 'Maria' *(see Maria)*.

Marjorie

The modern form of 'Margery' which was the usual form used throughout the Middle Ages of 'Margaret' *(see Margaret)*.

Marlene

German in origin, it is a contraction of 'Maria Magdalena' (Mary Magdalen), the full and proper name of Marlene Dietrich (1901–1992) the famous German film star *(see Madeleine)*.

Marsha

A variant spelling from the USA of 'Marcia' *(see Marcia)*.

Martha

From the Aramaic meaning 'lady' or 'mistress' it was the name of one of Christ's disciples, the sister of Lazarus and Mary (John 11:1; Luke 10:38).

Mary

The English form of the Hebrew name 'Miriam' meaning 'desired' or 'longed for'. It has been the most popular and enduring of all female names throughout Europe ('Marie' French; 'Maria' German; 'Marya' Russian). It was a popular name at the time of Christ; there was Mary of Magdala, Mary the mother James, Mary of Bethany. Its popularity in later centuries was due to Mary of Nazareth, the virgin mother of Jesus. It was common in the early centuries of Christianity, there being several saints who bore the name, but it dropped out of use for several hundred years as the name of the mother of Jesus was considered too holy to be used. It was not until the twelfth century that it gradually came back into use throughout Europe and grew, once again, in popularity. There are over 2000 churches dedicated to Mary, the mother of Jesus, throughout England alone. Many other female names are derived from 'Mary' *(see names commencing Mari-)*.

15 August

Matilda

The Latin form used in Britain from Norman times; derived from the German name 'Mathildis' meaning 'brave little maid'. The medieval vernacular form used alongside 'Matilda' was 'Maud'; both were common up until the fifteenth century. They dropped out of use, but enjoyed a revival in the eighteenth century. There was one saint who was the wife of the German king, Henry the Fowler. As a widow, she founded four famous German Benedictine monasteries (d.968).

14 March

Maud *(Maude)*

The English form of the German name 'Mathildis' and an alternative form to 'Matilda'. Borne by the wife of William the Conqueror, it was a popular Norman name. The Empress Maud (1102–1167) conducted a civil war in England in a quest for the throne; and Tennyson (1855) wrote a poem entitled *Maud*.

Maura

Of Celtic origin, its meaning is uncertain. There are six saints who bore the name, but little is known about any of them.

15 January

Maureen

The English form of the Irish name 'Mairin' which is derived from 'Maire', the Irish form of 'Mary' *(see Mary)*.

May

A modern name, from the late nineteenth century, being a pet name derived from 'Mary' or 'Margaret'. By the 1920s it had become an independent name.

Meg

Short form of 'Margaret' *(see Margaret)*.

Megan *(Meagan)*

The Welsh short form of 'Margaret' *(see Margaret)*.

Melanie

From the Greek *'melaina'* meaning 'dark' or 'black'. The English form comes from the Old French form of the Latin 'Melania'. There are two saints of this name, Melania the Elder (*c*.342–410) and her granddaughter, Melania the Younger (*c*.383–438). The name was probably introduced into England by the Protestant Hugenots. It dropped out of use for over a century and reappeared in the middle of the twentieth century.

8 June

Mercedes

A Spanish name derived from the title of the Virgin Mary, 'Maria de las Mercedes' (Mary of Mercies), when in Spain the name 'Mary' was considered too sacred to use; but as there was a popular devotion to the Blessed Virgin her titles were used. It is more frequently found in Spain, France and the USA than in Britain.

Mercia

A Latin form of 'Mercy' *(see Mercy)*.

Mercy

The seventeenth-century Puritans introduced this name, along with 'Faith', 'Hope' and 'Charity' to avoid using the traditional names associated with saints which they did not approve of. The name comes from *'merces'*, the Latin for 'reward'.

Michaela

The feminine form of 'Michael' *(see Michael)*.

Michelle

From the French feminine form of 'Michel' (Michael) *(see Michael)*.

Mildred

From the Old English 'Mildthryth' meaning 'gentle counsellor'. This is the name of a seventh-century (d.*c.*700) abbess of Minister, Isle of Thanet, Kent. Her mother and two sisters were also honoured, by popular acclaim, as saints. The name dropped out of use for several centuries, but was revived in the nineteenth century; but not often found in recent years.

13 July

Miriam

From the Hebrew (although it may originally have been Egyptian) meaning 'desired' or 'longed for'; the English form is 'Mary' *(see Mary)*. This was the name of the elder sister of Moses (Exodus 2:4–8; 15:20–21) and was a very popular name in first century Palestine at the time of Christ. It is still a favoured name in the Jewish community.

Moira *(Moyra)*

The English form of the Irish name 'Maire' which is the Irish version of 'Mary' *(see Mary)*.

Molly

The familiar form of 'Mary' *(see Mary)*.

Monica

Probably of African or Phoenician origin, as the saint from whom we get this name was born in Carthage in 332 AD. In the Middle Ages it was thought to have come from the Latin *'monere'* meaning 'to advise' or 'to warn', but this is unlikely. By her prayers and example St Monica converted her son, Augustine, who became one of the greatest thinkers and theologians; a saint and doctor of the Church.

27 August

N

Nancy
Its origins are uncertain but it first emerged as a familiar form of 'Ann'; then in the USA became an independent name *(see Ann)*.

Naomi
From the Hebrew meaning 'the pleasant one'. It was the name of Ruth's mother-in-law and her story can be found in the Book of Ruth. It was first used as a Christian name in the seventeenth century.

Natalie *(Nathalie)*
From the Latin *'natalis'* meaning 'birthday', referring to *'Natalis Domini'* (the birthday of the Lord – Christmas). Under its Latin form 'Natalia' there are three saints who bore the name. It has long been used in France and Germany, and not until the twentieth century in Britain.

1 December

Nell
The short form of 'Eleanor', e.g. Nell Gwyn's name was Eleanor Gwyn *(see Eleanor)*.

Nicola
The Italian feminine form (from the Latin) of 'Nicholas' *(see Nicholas)*.

Nicole
The French feminine form of 'Nicholas' *(see Nicholas)*.

Nina

The shortened Russian form of 'Ann' *(see Ann)*.

Ninette

A name which illustrates how international names have become. It is the French diminutive form of the Russian shortened form of 'Ann'. It came into the English-speaking world in the twentieth century, by way of France.

O

Odette

The French diminutive of 'Odille' which is the French form of the German name 'Otilia' meaning 'prosperous one'. There was one rather obscure saint of this name who died *c.*720.

13 December

Olga

A Russian name of Scandinavian origin derived from the Norse word *'helga'* meaning 'holy'. St Olga, wife of Igor, Duke of Kiev (879–969) was believed to be the first Russian to become a Christian.

11 July

Olivia *(Olive)*

Believed to come from the Latin *'oliva'* meaning 'olive'. There are two obscure saints of this name; apart from being virgin-martyrs of the first two centuries of Christianity, little is known about either of them. It can be considered as the female form of 'Oliver' *(see Oliver).*

5 March

P

Patience
As with the other names taken from the Christian virtues, like 'Faith', 'Hope' and 'Charity', it was introduced by the Puritans of the seventeenth century. It comes from the Latin word *'patientia'* meaning 'endurance', and probably derived from the verb *'patior'* meaning 'to suffer'. Patience is one of the seven Christian virtues.

Patricia
The feminine form of the Latin 'Patricius' *(see Patrick)*. There is an actual St Patricia (d.c.665), a virgin from Constantinople who became a nun at Rome and is one of the patrons of Naples.

(St Patrick) 17 March, (St Patricia) 25 August

Paula
The feminine form of the Latin, 'Paul' (see Paul). There are seven saints of this name; five of whom were martyrs dying for their faith in the early years of Christianity. One was a fourteenth-century nun and the last, the nineteenth-century saint, was the founder of a Religious Teaching Order of nuns.

(nineteenth century saint) 11 June

Paulette
A modern name originating from France and derived from 'Paula' *(see Paula)*.

Pauline

The French form of the Latin 'Paulina' which is the feminine of 'Paulinus'. There are twelve saints who bore the name 'Paulinus', the most prominent being St Paulinus of York (d.644) who converted and baptised King Edwin of Northumbria and thousands of his subjects. However, the name in the English-speaking world is commonly accepted as the female equivalent of 'Paul'.

(St Paulinus of York) 10 October, (St Paul) 29 June

Petra

From the Greek *'petra'* meaning 'stone' or 'rock'; this is the feminine form of 'Peter' *(see Peter)*.

Petrina

A feminine form of 'Peter' *(see Petra and Peter)*.

Philippa

The Latin feminine form of 'Philip' *(see Philip)*. Until modern times, women were actually called 'Philip' although this Latin form of the name did exist. It was particularly popular in early Christian times. There are four saintly women called 'Philippa'; the first saint was crucified with a group of martyrs at Perga, Pamphilia, in 220.

20 September

Philomena

Thought to be from the Greek verb *'philoumai'* meaning 'I am loved'. There was one St Philomena (d.c.500) venerated at Ancona, Italy, but nothing is known about her. In 1802, research appeared to have found a second saint; interest spread and the name became popular before further advanced research revealed an error and devotion to the 'saint' was prohibited in 1961.

5 July

Phoebe

From the Greek meaning 'the bright one'. St Paul in his letter to the Romans, commends Phoebe, a deaconess at Cenchreae near Corinth, to his readers (Romans 16:1–3). The name was introduced into England after the Reformation.

3 September

Pippa

A familiar form of 'Philippa' *(see Philippa)*.

Priscilla

From the Latin name meaning 'of ancient lineage'. Luke refers to a Priscilla who was the wife of Aquilla (Acts 18:2). The name was popular among the seventeenth-century Puritans who first introduced it to the English-speaking world.

8 July

Prudence

From the Latin word *'prudentia'* meaning 'prudence'; it can also be the feminine form of 'Prudentius'. There are two little-known male saints of this name and a female, 'Blessed Prudentia', a fifteenth-century Italian abbess. The name was very popular with the Puritans of the seventeenth century who took it to the USA.

6 May

R

Rachel *(Rachael)*

From the Hebrew meaning 'ewe'. It was the name of the wife of Jacob (Genesis 29:10) and mother of Joseph and Benjamin (Genesis 30:25). Always a popular Jewish name, it was not used in the Christian community until the Puritans of the seventeenth century adopted it.

Raquel

The Spanish form of 'Rachel' *(see Rachel)*.

Ramona

The feminine form of 'Raymond' *(see Raymond)*.

Rebecca

From the Latin form of the Hebrew name 'Rebekah', which is probably of Aramaic origin; its meaning is unknown. It was the name of Isaac's wife (Genesis 24:45) and mother of Jacob. Always popular in the Jewish community, it became equally popular as a Christian name after the Reformation.

Regina

From the Latin word *'regina'* meaning 'queen'. There was a St Regina (d.286) a virgin-martyr of Autun, but the name's use comes from the popular title of the Virgin Mary, 'Regina Coeli' (Queen of Heaven) that all medieval Christians would have heard and prayed.

Reine

The French form of 'Regina' *(see Regina)*.

Renee

A French name which comes from the Latin *'renatus'* meaning 'born again'. For the Christians of the early centuries of Christianity, this was a significant baptismal (or christening) name, for by baptism the Christian is 'born again' (John 3:7). There were two saints called 'Renatus', the better known being St Renatus (Rene) Goupil (d.1642) tortured and clubbed to death by the Iroquois Indians of North America.

19 October

Rhoda

From the Greek for 'rose'. It was the name of a very minor New Testament character (Acts 12:13). It was first used in the English-speaking world by the seventeenth-century Puritans.

Richelle

A modern French feminine form of 'Richard' *(see Richard)*.

Rita

Before it became an independent name, this was the short form of the Spanish 'Margarita' (Margaret) *(see Margaret)*.

Roberta

A Latin form of 'Robert' used as the feminine version of the name *(see Robert)*.

Rosalie

From the Latin *'rosalia'* referring to a garland of roses. There was a St Rosalia (d.1160), a Sicilian recluse who became the patron saint of Palermo, Sicily.

15 July

Rose

The Latin is *'rosa'* (rose) but the name seems not to have originated from the Latin but from the German. The common medieval form of the name was 'Rohesia' or 'Roese'. There are two saints of this name; the better known St Rose of Lima (1586–1617), the first American-born to be canonised as a saint; she is the patron of South America.

23 August

Rosemary

A name which first appeared in the eighteenth century and was popular in the nineteenth century, probably due to the Romantic movement in literature. At a time when flower names were in vogue (like 'Rose', 'Lily') it was probably taken from the herb. However, some see it as the combination of the names 'Rose' and 'Mary' *(see Rose and Mary)*.

Rosie

A familiar form of 'Rose' or 'Rosemary' *(see Rose and Rosemary)*.

Ruth

The name of the biblical character whose story is told in the Book of Ruth . She was a Moabite and the meaning of her name is unknown. It was first used as a Christian name in the seventeenth century and was very popular among the Puritans who introduced it into the USA.

S

Sabina

The feminine form of the Latin name 'Sabinus'. The Sabines were a tribal people conquered by the early Romans ('The Sabine women' is a subject in classical art). There were ten saints of the early Christian centuries named 'Sabinus', and two women martyrs called 'Sabina'.

29 August

Sadie

A familiar form of 'Sarah' *(see Sarah)*.

Sally

Originally this was a familiar form of 'Sarah'; however, in the twentieth century it has become an independent name *(see Sarah)*.

Sara *(Sarah)*

From the Hebrew meaning 'princess'. It is the name of Abram's (later Abraham) wife (Genesis 11:29). At first it is spelt 'Sarai' meaning 'contentious'; later (Genesis 17:15) God ordered her to be called 'Sarah'. The name was not used in England until the twelfth century, when it was spelt 'Sarra'. The modern spelling appeared in the seventeenth century when the name was used extensively by the Puritans.

Seraphina

The Latin feminine form of the Hebrew word *'seraphim'* meaning 'noble' or 'ardent believer'. It is one of the orders of angels (Isaiah 6:2). There are two saints of this name in the Christian calendar; neither of them well known.

12 March

Serena

The feminine form of the Latin *'serenus'* meaning 'calm' or 'serene'. According to early, and unreliable records, St Serena (d.*c*.290) was the wife of the Emperor Diocletian. A second saint of this name (also known as 'Fina') lived in Tuscany (d.1253) and was famed for her great patience in extreme pain and adversity.

16 August

Sharon

This name has been both male and female over the centuries. It first appeared among the Puritans of the seventeenth century, who searched the Bible for new Christian names, when they rejected all traditional names. They found a place name in the Bible (The Song of Songs 2:1) 'I am the rose of Sharon' (on the coastal plain in northern Palestine) and used it.

Sharona

Latin style form of 'Sharon' *(see Sharon)*.

Sidony

From the Latin feminine form of the name 'Sidonius', meaning 'a man from Sidon' (a Phoenician town). Two saints bore this male name, the most important being St Sidonius Apollinaris (*c*.423–480) who as bishop of Clermont, saved his people from the invading Goths. The name is also associated with the Greek *'sindon'* meaning 'winding sheet', referring to the burial cloth of Christ, the Shroud of Turin.

21 August

Silvia

The original spelling of 'Sylvia' from the Latin for 'wood'. According to legend 'Rhea Silvia' was the name of the mother of the twins, Romulus and Remus, who founded the city of Rome. It was also the name of the saintly mother of one of Rome's most influential popes, St Gregory the Great (d.604). Among many things, he sent Augustine (596) to convert England.

3 November

Sophia

From the Greek for 'wisdom'. Two third-century martyrs bore the name; a third was the legendary mother of three sisters, 'Faith', 'Hope' and 'Charity' who died as martyrs in the Roman arena. It was later discovered that the account was not historical but allegory, recorded to teach how the virtues spring from *'Hagia Sophia'* (holy wisdom).

30 September

Sophie

The French form of 'Sophia' *(see Sophia)*.

Stella

From the Latin word for *'star'*. First used in the sixteenth century, it has since been used in the Roman Catholic community as derived from the title 'Stella Maris' (Star of the Sea), an ancient title accorded to the Virgin Mary.

Stephanie

From the Latin 'Stephania', used by the early Christian community as the feminine form of 'Stephen'; who was highly regarded as the first Christian martyr, stoned to death in the first Jewish persecution of the incipient Church (Acts 7:54).

26 December

Sue

The short form of 'Susan' or 'Susanna' *(see Susanna)*.

Susanna *(Susannah)*

From the Hebrew meaning 'lily'. There were four shadowy saints who bore this name, but it was the story of sexual treachery and the heroism of Susanna in the apocryphal Book of Daniel and Susanna, that caught popular Christian imagination in the early centuries of the Church (and inspired some of the great artists). It was particularly popular in medieval England.

18 January

Sylvia

Altenative spelling of 'Silvia' *(see Silvia)*.

T

Tabitha

This is the Aramaic equivalent of 'Dorcas' meaning 'gazelle' or 'graceful'. It was the name of the woman that was restored to life by Peter (Acts 9:32–43) *(see Dorcas)*.

Talitha

From the Aramaic meaning 'little girl'. As a Christian name, it is derived from the Aramaic words of Jesus to the apparently dead twelve year old, 'Talitha kum' (little girl get up – Mark 5:41).

Tamara

A Russian name derived from the Hebrew 'Tamar' meaning 'date palm'. There are three biblical women with this ancient name: the wife of Er, son of Judah (Genesis 38:6); a daughter of David (1 Chronicles 3:9); a beautiful daughter of Absalom (2 Samuel 14:27).

Tamsin

A shortened form of 'Thomasina' which in medieval times was popular as the feminine form of 'Thomas' *(see Thomas)*.

Teresa *(Theresa)*

A common, and popular name found throughout Europe, but its origin and meaning is obscure. It is first found in the fifth century in the form 'Therasia', belonging to the wife of St Paulinus, bishop of Nola. Later its use spread through the fame of the great

Spanish mystic St Teresa of Avila (1515–1582) whose reforms of religious life in Spain and mystical writings had a powerful effect for centuries (a). There have been three other saints, including the very popular St Thérèse of Lisieux ('The Little Flower'), (1873–1897) a young Carmelite nun, whose short life and writings have made her the most popular female saint of modern times and gained her the rare title of Doctor of the Church; and also the saintly and hugely admired Blessed Teresa of Calcutta, better known as Mother Teresa, (1910–1997) famed for the total gift of herself to the desperately poor and dying of Calcutta and beyond (b).

(a) 15 October, (b) 1 October

Terri

A modern shortened form of 'Teresa' or a feminine form of 'Terry', the shortened form of 'Terence' *(see Teresa or Terence)*.

Tessa

A familiar form of 'Teresa' *(see Teresa)*.

Thea

A shortened form of 'Dorothea' *(see Dorothea)*.

Thecla

Derived from the Greek name 'Theokleia' meaning 'divine follower'. It was the name of a first-century saint (there are six other little-known saints) who, according to a very unreliable source, was a follower of St Paul and the first Christian martyr.

23 September

Theodora

From the Greek meaning 'gift of God'. (Another version of 'Dorothy'). It is also the feminine form of 'Theodore' *(see Theodore)*. There are seven saints of this name, the best known being the Empress Theodora, wife of Theophilus (d.867), who struggled to restore the veneraton of icons in the Eastern Church.

1 April

Therese

The French form of 'Teresa' *(see Teresa)*. Associated, in the Roman Catholic community, with St Therese of Lisieux, the young Carmelite nun (1873–1897) whose autobiography, *The Story of a Soul*, made her the most famous saint of modern times and a doctor of the Church.

1 October

U

Ursula

From the Latin *'ursa'* meaning 'she-bear'. The story of the fourth-century St Ursula, and her virgin companions who died for the Christian faith at Cologne, was one of the most popular of the Middle Ages; and the use of the name was widespread.

21 October

V

Valerie

The French form of the Latin 'Valeria', the feminine form of 'Valerius', probably derived from *'valere'* meaning 'healthy' and 'strong'. There are three very obscure early Christian martyrs of this name in the Christian calendar.

28 April

Vera

From the Russian word *'vjera'* meaning 'faith'. It is the same as the Latin feminine form of *'verus'* meaning 'true'. The name has only been used in the last hundred years in the English-speaking world.

Verity

From the Latin word *'veritas'* meaning 'truth'. It was a popular name among the Puritans of the seventeenth century.

Veronica

Derived from combining two Latin words *'verus'* meaning 'true' and *'iconicus'* meaning 'image'. The name was given to a cloth which was believed to carry the image of Christ's face. According to legend, a woman in the crowd (later called 'Veronica') wiped the face of Jesus as he carried his cross to Calvary. The Eastern Church identifies the woman as the one healed in Matthew 9:20–22.

Victoria

The feminine form of 'Victor' from the Latin *'victorius'* meaning 'victory'. It was hardly known in England before 1837 and the accession of Queen Victoria; however, there are two martyrs of early Christian times of this name.

23 December

Vivian *(Vivien)*

A name which has been used by both genders. It originates from Latin *'vivatus'* and means 'full of life'. There was a martyr called 'Viviana' (also known as 'Bibiana') who according to unsubstantiated legend, was scourged to death for her faith, in fourth-century Rome.

2 December

Winifred *(Winefred)*

The English form of the Welsh name 'Gwenfrewi' meaning 'peaceful friend'. The seventh-century Welsh saint of this name was a historical person, but her life has been so decorated with legends, that little is known for sure. She was a martyr and associated with the Holy Well (at Holywell) to which for many centuries pilgrimages have been made and cures claimed.

3 November

Y

Yolanda *(Yolande)*

Of very uncertain origin and meaning. There was a saintly Hungarian woman (d.1298) of this name who was the daughter of King Bela IV of Hungary, and a niece of St Elizabeth of Hungary.

15 June

Z

Zillah

From the Hebrew meaning 'shade'. It is the name of one of Lamech's wives (Genesis 4:19). It was introduced into Britain – and later into the USA – by the seventeenth-century Puritans, in their search for new Christian names.

Zita

The origins of this name are obscure; it is believed to come from medieval Tuscany because the saint (1218–1272), from whom we get the name, was from that part of Italy. She lived and died a domestic servant but was outstanding in sanctity. St Zita is the patron saint of those engaged in domestic work.

27 April

Zoe

From the Greek meaning 'life'. In the Septuagint (Greek) translation of the Hebrew Bible, the name 'Eve' was translated as 'Zoe'. It was a common Christian name in Byzantine times and there are two little-known saints from that period. It was not used in England until the nineteenth century.

5 July

www.ingramcontent.com/pod-product-compliance
Lightning Source LLC
Chambersburg PA
CBHW020411080526
44584CB00014B/1278